The Princeton Review

Cracking

THE
GOLDEN STATE
EXAMINATION

Geometry

by Oliver Butterick and Rick Sliter

Random House, Inc.
New York
www.randomhouse.com/princetonreview

The Independent Education Consultants Association recognizes The Princeton Review as a valuable resource for high school and college students applying to college and graduate school.

Princeton Review, L.L.C.
2315 Broadway
New York, NY 10024

E-mail: comments@review.com

Published in the United States by Random House, Inc., New York.

ISBN 0-375-75353-2

Editor: Lesly Atlas
Production Editor: Kristen Azzara
Production Coordinator: Jennifer Arias
Designer: Greta Englert

Manufactured in the United States of America

9 8 7 6 5 4 3 2 1

First Edition

ACKNOWLEDGMENTS

Thank you to all who encouraged me through the process of writing this book, including Brooke Butterick, Tiffany Simons, Erik Sincoff, Snehal Naik, Anjali Bal, Amanda Allen, James Gallardo, Jen Snell, Sam Floyd, Greta Schuman, Jeff Lewis, and Brenda Andrews. Thanks to all the people at The Princeton Review who helped to make this book a reality: Lesly Atlas, Kristen Azzara, the TPR production staff, especially Scott Harris, Sionainn Marcoux for her expert review of this book, and especially Rick Sliter, for believing in me, and for providing me with invaluable advice and revisions.

Special thanks go out to Leo Haertling and Marty Butterick. Your friendship and confidence in me have given me the motivation to take on this endeavor and many others in the past. I owe this success, and many more to come, to the both of you.

Extra special thanks to Laura Anne Hardaker, without whom this book would never have been finished. Thanks for your support throughout the entire process. I hope this is but the first of many books we will write together.

To anyone whom I may have forgotten: Know that you are appreciated and that I could not have done this alone. Hi Mom and Bruce and Dad and Bette.

Contents

THE MYSTERY EXAM: ABOUT THE GOLDEN STATE EXAMINATIONS

WHAT ARE THE GOLDEN STATE EXAMS?

Golden State Examinations (GSEs) were established by the State of California Board of Education in 1983 (so your parents never took them—they have probably even never heard of them and may not understand how important they are!). The tests are designed to offer a rigorous examination in key academic subjects to students in grades 7–12. Students who receive recognition have a variety of advantages over those who don't—including the fact that their school transcript will be more attractive to college admissions boards.

The GSE program has grown in the last few years, both in the number of different exams offered and the number of students who take at least one GSE. During the 1999–2000 academic year, thirteen different GSE exams will be administered, and California students will complete over 1 million examinations. In 1998, more than 2,100 graduates earned the Golden State Seal Merit Diploma, which recognizes students who have mastered their high school curriculum (see below for more information on the Merit Diploma).

You probably purchased this book because a teacher recommended it or because you were told to get ready to take a GSE. Well, lucky for you, this is the most complete guide you can own to prepare for the Golden State Examinations. Our goal is simple—to get you ready for the Golden State Examination in Geometry.

WE'RE HERE TO HELP

Like we said earlier, the Golden State Examinations are somewhat of a mystery to students, particularly because there aren't any official practice tests that you can study from. We're here to change all that. Our research and development team has spent countless hours to ensure that this guide tells you everything you need to know to ace the Golden State Examinations. All of the information that's released about the GSEs is included in this book. We've also spoken to students and teachers about their experiences with these tests and designed our content review around their feedback. In short, we have the inside scoop on the Golden State Examinations, and we're going to share it with you.

What's So Special about This Book?

Golden State Examinations test subject knowledge, as well as the application of that knowledge. The goal of this book is two-fold. First, we want to help you remember or relearn some of the key components and subject material that's covered in the exam. Second, we want you to become familiar with the structure of the GSE, so that you'll know exactly what to do on test day.

We at The Princeton Review aren't big fans of standardized tests, and we understand the stress and challenge that a GSE presents. But with our techniques and some work on your part, you should be able to do well on these tests. There's just one more thing you might be wondering—why *should* I take the Golden State Examinations?

WHY SHOULD YOU TAKE THE GOLDEN STATE EXAMINATIONS?

There are many reasons why you should spend time and energy getting ready for the GSEs. They include:

- **Qualification for a Golden State Merit Diploma**
  The Golden State Merit Diploma is one of the—if not *the*—highest academic awards given by the State of California. In the pages that follow, we will detail exactly how you can qualify for a Merit Diploma.

- **Recognition on Your Transcript**
  If you perform well on a Golden State Examination, you will receive recognition on your high school transcript. We'll tell you how the scoring system and award processes work in the pages that follow.

- **College Admissions Committees Will Love You!**
  A strong performance on the Golden State Examinations will make you look great to colleges and universities; they're academic awards that will demonstrate to schools that you can excel in an academic environment.

- **They Are Risk Free!**
  First, there is absolutely no fee to take a Golden State Examination, so you won't need to worry about spending money on these tests. Second, there is absolutely no penalty if you do not perform well on a Golden State Examination. A score that does not give you an award will not appear on your transcript. In fact, only you will know if you did *not* receive recognition for a Golden State Examination. So, you've got nothing to lose, and a lot to gain!

- **All the Things Your Teacher Would Say:**
  There are academic benefits of the tests as well. If you asked your teacher why you should take these exams, your teacher would probably tell you that, in addition to all the benefits listed above, "These tests provide a great opportunity for you to demonstrate what you have learned throughout high school, with the possibility of receiving numerous awards and titles for strong academic performance. The Golden State Examinations are a challenge that can enrich your high school experience."

Although we'll be a little less formal in the way we say it, we agree with the teacher's advice. The GSEs are your chance to show off what you know. You should receive recognition for all your hard work, and we're going to give you every tool we can to ensure that you do well!

HOW ARE STUDENTS RECOGNIZED FOR THEIR PERFORMANCE?

If you score within the highest levels on any one Golden State Examination, you will receive one of three awards: high honors, honors, or recognition. Say you take three GSEs, one in history, one in biology, and one in written composition. Because you used The Princeton Review test-prep books, you can give yourself a pat on the back! You are among the one-third of all students who pass the GSEs, earning scores as listed below:

Test	Award
Written Composition	High Honors
History	Honors
Biology	Recognition

These awards are formally called Academic Excellence Awards. This means that students who receive one of these three awards will receive an Academic Excellence Award from the State of California. This will be recorded on your high school transcript, and you'll receive a gold insignia on your diploma if you get a score of high honors or honors.

Here are the three levels of honors given on the GSE and what they mean:

- **High Honors**—This is the most prestigious award given to students on the Geometry GSE. It will be given to about the top 10 percent of students. If you receive "high honors" on the Geometry GSE, you will receive a special gold seal on your high school diploma and the award will be placed on your transcript. Further, you can use this result as part of the requirements necessary for pursuing the ultimate award, the Golden State Merit Diploma.

- **Honors**—This is the second most prestigious award given to students on the Geometry GSE. It will be given to about 12 percent of the students that take the exam (students who score in the 78th to 90th percentile). If you receive "honors" on the Geometry GSE, you will receive the same rewards as students who achieved a score of "high honors."

- **Recognition**—This is the final type of Academic Excellence award given to students on the Geometry GSE. It will be given to approximately fifteen percent of the students that take the exam (students who score in the 66th to 78th percentiles). If you get a "recognition" on the Geometry GSE, you will receive notification of this achievement on your high school transcript. Further, you can use this as part of the requirements necessary for pursuing the ultimate award, the Golden State Seal Merit Diploma.

Any one of these awards signals high achievement to colleges, universities, and employers. Finally, Golden State scholars are eligible to pursue a Golden State Seal Merit Diploma.

What Is the Golden State Seal Merit Diploma?

In July of 1996, the State of California developed a Golden State Seal Merit Diploma program to recognize high school graduates who demonstrated high performance in several different academics areas. The Golden State Seal Merit Diploma is the most prestigious award you can receive by taking Golden State Examinations. In 1997, the first year that the Golden State Seal Merit Diploma was issued, more than 1,300 high school seniors received the award. This number jumped to more than 2,100 in 1998, and will continue to increase as more students take Golden State Examinations.

In order to receive the Merit Diploma, students must receive high honors, honors, or recognition designations on *six* different Golden State Examinations. The specific tests and requirements are described below.

How Can You Get a Golden State Seal Merit Diploma?

You do **not** need to apply to receive a Golden State Merit Diploma. You just need to complete four required examinations, plus two elective exams, and receive at least recognition for them. School districts track the performance of each student and submit the information to the California Department of Education.

The four exams that students must pass are:

1. English (Written Composition or Reading and Literature)
2. U.S. History
3. Mathematics (Algebra, Geometry, or High School Mathematics)
4. Science (Biology, Chemistry, Physics, or Coordinated Science)

In addition to the four required exams, you will take **two** other GSEs selected from the following: Economics, Spanish Language, or Government and Civics. You may also complete an *additional* science, mathematics, or English exam as one of your two electives. For example, let's say you complete both the Algebra and Geometry examinations, and receive Academic Excellence awards on each exam. In this case, one of them will be counted as the mathematics *required* exam; the other will be counted as an elective.

What Material Is Covered on the GSE?

Golden State Examinations are developed by a committee of teachers, university professors, and other education specialists. Each examination is designed and tested so that the content reflects the state standards for each subject. In general, you should expect that the information tested on a GSE will be similar to what you've been tested on during the academic year. The style and format of the GSE may be different, but the material should be just like the stuff you studied in class. Unlike many other high school examinations, the GSEs are not designed to trick or trap you.

Most examinations consist of one day of multiple-choice questions, followed by one day of written work. All Golden State Examinations consist of two 45-minute parts. In chapter 2, we'll discuss the specific format, structure, and scoring of the Geometry Golden State Examination.

SO HERE'S THE DEAL

Below are frequently asked questions about the administration of the GSEs. If there's anything we don't cover or if you're still confused, ask your guidance counselor or teacher.

How are GSE Exams Scored?

Every Golden State Examination has specific scoring criteria based on its format, structure, and level of difficulty. See chapter 2 for more specific information about how the Geometry GSE is scored.

As we mentioned, there is no penalty whatsoever for poor performance on a Golden State Examination. If you fail to receive one of the honors designations we discussed earlier, there will be no mention of it on your academic transcript. Further, students who do not receive an honors designation on one GSE should still be encouraged to take additional GSEs. Each test is scored independently—performance on one GSE will have no impact on the scoring of any other GSE.

When Will You Receive Your GSE Results?

Results from the Golden State Examinations are first sent to your school district. If you take a winter examination, you should expect to hear about your results in May. If you take a spring examination, you should expect to hear about your results once you return to school in the fall. If you have any questions regarding your performance on the GSE, you can talk to your high school counselor for some more information about it.

> Remember only about one-third of all test takers are honored for their performance on the Golden State Examination. This means that two-thirds don't pass and receive no recognition! These tests aren't a shoo-in; you need to know the material and be familiar with the structure to pass. This book is your key to being among the well prepared.

Can I Take the Test More Than Once?

No. Students are eligible to take each GSE only one time. For this reason, be sure that you are prepared to take each Golden State Examination. If you're holding this book, you're well on your way!

How Can I Keep Track of All of the GSE Tests and Requirements?

Determining which GSEs to take, and when to take them, can be a confusing process. The California Department of Education has designed some worksheets for use by students that will help you keep track of this information. Ask your high school counselor for a copy of these worksheets.

How Do I Inform Colleges about My Golden State Awards?

If you are applying to a college, university, or military academy, you will want to make sure that any awards you've received on the Golden State Examinations are included in your application. If you received high honors, honors, or recognition on a GSE, this will be noted on your high school transcript. In addition to this, you can get a form called the *GSE Status Report for College Applications*. This form is available from your high school counselor; along with your high school transcript, it will ensure that admissions boards notice your performance on the tests.

For additional information about the GSE program, contact the Standards, Curriculum, and Assessment Division of the California Department of Education:

Phone: (916) 657-3011

Fax: (916) 657-4964

E-mail: star@cde.ca.gov

Internet: www.cde.ca.gov/cilbranch/sca/gse/gse.html

HOW THIS BOOK IS ORGANIZED

The next chapter of this book is devoted to giving you the specifics about the test you are about to take. We will discuss test structure, format, and scoring, and we'll also talk about some techniques and strategies that can be helpful to you. Our goal is to provide you with a "bag of tricks" that you can use throughout this exam.

We will then provide a specific content review of the subject material that's covered on the GSE. Rather than giving you lists of things to know, our goal is to give you information so that you can apply it to the specific way it's asked on the GSE. How do we know what is tested on the Golden State Examinations? We have carefully studied California State Curriculum Standards and Golden State Examination questions, surveyed high school teachers, and reviewed textbooks to determine exactly what is covered on each test. We'll use sample questions throughout the review to show you how certain topics are tested on the GSE.

Finally, we have prepared and constructed four full-length practice tests for the Golden State Examination. We will provide you with detailed explanations to each problem, and sample written work when appropriate. Use these tests to recognize the areas in which you need improvement.

WHAT IS THE PRINCETON REVIEW?

The Princeton Review is the nation's leader in test preparation. We have offices in more than fifty cities across the country, as well as many outside the United States. The Princeton Review supports more than 2 million students every year with our courses, books, on-line services, and software programs. In addition to helping high school students prepare for the GSEs, we help them with the SAT-I, SAT-II, PSAT, and ACT, along with many other statewide standardized tests. The Princeton Review's strategies and techniques are unique, and most of all, successful.

Remember, this book will work best in combination with the material you have learned throughout your high school course. Our goals are to help you remember what you have been taught over the past year, and show you how to apply this knowledge to the specific format and structure of the Golden State Examination.

AND FINALLY...

We applaud your efforts to spend the time and energy to prepare for the Golden State Examination in Geometry. You are giving yourself the opportunity to be rewarded for your academic achievement. Remember that the Golden State Examinations are not designed to test you on information you have never seen before. A strong year in your academic subject, combined with a review of the material and test-taking strategies in this book, will leave you more than prepared to handle the GSE. Don't become frustrated if you don't remember everything at once; it may take some time for the information and skills to come back. Stay focused, practice, and try to have fun working through this book. And finally, good luck!

STRUCTURE AND STRATEGIES

It may seem pretty intimidating that only one-third of all students who take the GSEs receives any sort of honors. You might be wondering whether or not you can be one of them . . . but of course you can! Just remember that most students don't prepare at all before taking the Golden State Examinations, so you're already ahead of the game.

In this chapter, we'll tell you exactly which geometry concepts are tested, and how. We'll also give you an idea of the scoring process, and the structure and format of the test. Most importantly, we'll introduce you to some solid GSE test-taking techniques. It's crucial that you use our techniques when you're taking the test. We'll refer to these throughout the book to make sure you incorporate them into your practice.

WHAT IS TESTED ON THE GEOMETRY GSE?

The content of the Geometry GSE is in alignment with the State Board *California Mathematics Academic Content Standards*. This means that what is tested on the Geometry GSE will be similar to the information you were presented during the academic year. The following is a breakdown of the content areas that may be covered:

- Geometry Basics

  —You will be tested on basic relationships and rules that deal with angles, lines, planes, triangle inequalities, and exterior angles.

- Special Triangles

  —In addition to the basics of triangles, you will be tested on specific triangle rules. Some of these rules include the Pythagorean Theorem, similar triangles, congruence, equilateral and isosceles triangles, and special triangle relationships.

- Polygon Properties

  —Other than triangles, you will be asked to perform calculations about quadrilaterals, and polygons with five or more sides. You will need to know relationships within polygons—sides, angles, midpoints, diagonals, and so forth.

- Area, Perimeter, and Circumference

  —You will need to know various geometric rules like perimeter, area, and circumference for all figures.

- Circle Properties

  —All basic definitions and rules about circles will be tested, including area, circumference, vectors, and arcs.

- Trigonometric Relationships

  —Certain trigonometry relationships such as sine, cosine, and tangent will be tested. If you have not yet taken trigonometry, don't worry. We'll cover the trigonometry basics that may appear on the Geometry GSE.

- Coordinate Geometry

  —Linear and nonlinear equations will be tested, including parabolas and hyperbolas.

- Transformations

  —Be prepared to solve questions that ask about translations, reflections, rotations, and dilations of geometric figures.

- Three-dimensional Properties and Relationships

  —Surface area, volume, and properties of diagonals will be tested.

- Geometric Probability

  —Probability questions can include both the two-dimensional model and the three-dimensional model.

In the chapters ahead, we will cover each of the topics mentioned above. We will provide substantial review in each of the topic areas that will be covered on the Geometry GSE.

HOW IS THE GEOMETRY GSE EXAM STRUCTURED?

The Golden State Examination in Geometry is a two-part examination, administered in two 45-minute sections.

Part I consists of approximately 30–35 multiple-choice questions. These questions are designed to test a wide range of geometric concepts. You will probably find several of these questions easy. You may find that you are unfamiliar with the concepts in some questions. Don't worry, we'll review all the material you need to know.

In general, these multiple-choice questions emphasize the concepts and principles of geometry. Each of these questions consists of four answer choices. Later, we'll talk about how to use the answer choices to your advantage.

Part II usually consists of gridded-response and written-response questions. The gridded-response questions require you to solve problems, and there will be no answer choices to choose from. You'll need to fill in your responses on a grid found on your answer sheet. We'll cover gridded-response questions throughout this book. The written-response portion of Part II requires that you apply your mathematical skills. It's sort of like a "geometry essay." You will be given a problem that involves several steps, and you'll be asked to write out a correct solution. You will be evaluated based on the explanations that accompany the solution, as well as the solution itself. This will be one area where you need to show your work in order to receive total credit.

HOW IS THE TEST SCORED?

A machine will score all of Part I and the gridded-response questions in Part II. Mathematics teachers and other professionals will score the written response portion of the Geometry GSE. Your performance on Part I combined with your performance on Part II of the Geometry GSE will determine your overall score.

CAN I USE A CALCULATOR ON THIS TEST?

Yes! A scientific or graphing calculator is required for some of the problems that are given on the Geometry GSE. You should use the calculator that you have used throughout your math classes. You can use any calculator you want, except for ones with QWERTY (typewriter) keyboards.

WHERE CAN I FIND A REAL GSE EXAM?

Sample copies of the real GSEs are not available, but you should get enough practice from the four full-length diagnostic Geometry Golden State Exams in the back of this book, which are followed by explanations and sample student written-responses. These tests simulate the format and kinds of questions you can expect to see on the GSE.

YOUR BAG OF TRICKS

Have you ever seen the cartoon *Felix the Cat*? Felix fought crime, solved problems, and got his way out of difficult situations by reaching into his bag of tricks. In this special bag, he'd find the exact tool he needed to resolve any situation. With his bag of tricks, Felix was invincible.

We are going to help you fill up your own "bag of tricks." What will be in there? Strategies and tools for handling each type of question on the Geometry GSE, as well as general strategies for how to approach the test. It is important to know that being a smart test-taker is just as important as knowing the material tested. Managing your time, knowing when to guess, and knowing what the questions are *really* asking are skills you can learn, and we'll teach them to you. As you'll see, there is a difference between knowing the material, and *applying* it to the test.

Let's take an example of two students, Gretchen and Laurie, each with the same amount of geometry knowledge. Now, Gretchen took the same math class as Laurie, but Gretchen has received additional training. She has learned to think like the people who write the GSE; she understands their traps, quick ways to eliminate incorrect answer choices, and the best techniques to use for certain types of problems. In short, she has learned how to become a solid test taker. Gretchen, with her bag of tricks, is now going to do much better on the GSE than Laurie. Why? Not because she knows more, but because she knows how to take this specific test in a smarter way than Laurie does. She understands the rules of the game. Once you know the rules of the game, you know how best to apply your skills to the game.

General Strategies

Now that you know what is tested on the Geometry GSE, and in what format it is tested, we need to talk about the best way to take this test. In the pages that follow, we'll discuss some general tools for you to use as you proceed through the test. In the chapters ahead, we will discuss specific strategies for particular types of questions. For now, we're going to arm you with some general tools to put in *your* bag of tricks to use throughout the test. Using these can help you become a better GSE test taker.

An Empty Scantron Sheet Is a Bad Scantron Sheet

In the past, you've probably taken a standardized test that had a guessing penalty. This penalty means that points would be subtracted from your raw score if you answered a question incorrectly. Guessing penalties are meant to discourage test takers from answering every question. But guess what? There is NO guessing penalty on the GSE! Your score is only determined by the number of questions that you get correct; it doesn't matter how many questions you get incorrect. So, when you take the GSE, there is one thing that you must do before you turn in your test: **You must answer every single multiple-choice question.** There are about thirty questions on Part I of the Geometry GSE. Before you turn in your test, make sure that you have selected an answer for all thirty. Earning an Academic Excellence Award may boil down to just one additional point, and leaving a question blank guarantees a wrong answer.

Now you know that you must choose an answer for every question. Great, now let's talk about how to be an intelligent guesser.

 Process of Elimination (POE)

Try the following question:

What is the capital of Malawi?

Unsure? Do you even know where Malawi is located? If not, don't panic. Geography and world capitals are not topics tested on the GSE (especially the Geometry test!). If you had to answer this question without any answer choices, you'd probably be in trouble. You'd just randomly pick a city, and most likely guess wrong.

Of course, on the GSE, you will have answer choices to choose from. Rather than closing your eyes and selecting an answer at random, take a look at the choices—you might find some information that can help you:

What is the capital of Malawi?

A) Paris

B) Lilongwe

C) New York

D) London

Now do you know? Can you identify any answer choices that you *know* are not correct? Well, you can probably eliminate A, C, and D. Although you probably didn't know that Lilongwe was the capital of Malawi, you could tell that it was the correct answer by eliminating incorrect answer choices. This procedure is called Process of Elimination, or POE for short.

Process of Elimination will help you become a better guesser. This is because, often, it is easier to spot incorrect answer choices than it is to pinpoint the correct one. Remember to *cross out* any answer choice that you know is incorrect; then, if you still need to make a guess, select an answer from your remaining choices.

It is unlikely that POE will actually help you eliminate three answer choices like we did in the sample problem above. However, every time you get rid of one answer choice, the odds of getting that question correct go up significantly. Instead of a 25-percent chance of guessing correctly, you might find yourself guessing with a 50-percent (1 in 2) or 33-percent (1 in 3) chance of getting a question right.

Let's try another example that would be more likely to appear on the Geometry GSE:

> What polygon is created by the lines $x + 2y = 3$, $x + 2y = 4$, the x-axis, and the y-axis?
>
> A. triangle
>
> B. rectangle
>
> C. parallelogram
>
> D. trapezoid

Let's examine the situation. There are four distinct lines in the graph, so answer (A) can be eliminated, because triangles only have three lines. Next, you know that the x-axis and the y-axis intersect at a right angle. So, if a parallelogram were formed, the parallelogram would also be a rectangle (since rectangles are just parallelograms with right angles). Therefore, you can eliminate option (C). So, you are left with (B) rectangle (a figure with four right angles), and (D) trapezoid (a figure that can contain non-right angles). By converting one of the lines to slope-intercept format, you will see that it is not perpendicular to either the x-axis or the y-axis. Therefore, answer (B) can be eliminated, and you are left with the correct answer (D). At worst, if you forgot about slope-intercept, or didn't know if the line was perpendicular or not, your guess would be a one-in-two chance. Again, using POE will get you more points on the GSE.

Process of Elimination is such an important concept that we'll be referring to it throughout this book, including in the explanations provided to the practice tests. There are some specific POE strategies for certain geometry questions that will be presented in the chapters ahead. It is important that you practice using POE, because getting rid of incorrect answers is a powerful tool on the GSE.

So, I'll Just Start With #1 and Finish With #30, Right?

Some tests contain an order of difficulty within each section. On these kinds of tests, the first question is generally very easy, and the questions become progressively more difficult, with the last few questions being the hardest. On the Geometry GSE, however, there is no order of difficulty on the multiple-choice section of the exam. So, doing the test straight through, from 1 to 30, may not be your best strategy. Your goal on the test is to work as rapidly as you can without sacrificing accuracy. This means that if you find that a question is difficult for you, leave that one for later, and move on to another question.

 ## The Two-Pass System

Have you ever been given a question that stumped you, but you were sure you could solve it? Have you ever said, "Just one more minute. I know I can figure this out!" Well, we all have, and we all know that one more minute sometimes means five more minutes, and often, we don't end up with the right answer at all.

Don't let one question ruin your whole day. You've got a certain number of questions to tackle, and allowing one to throw off your timing might set you back. Here is a general rule for the multiple-choice section: *If you haven't figured out the correct answer in 90 seconds, skip the question and come back to it later.* We're not telling you to give up on it—if you can't answer the question, make a small mark on your answer sheet so you can come back to it later. After you complete the section, go back to the questions you weren't able to solve. Remember to use POE on these questions. Make sure you have selected an answer choice for every question before time is up.

We call this strategy the two-pass system. The first time you go through a section, try every question. If a question seems too difficult or stumps you, move on. Once you've completed the section, go back to those questions. If you still aren't sure how to solve, use POE and make a guess.

Often, when you go back to a problem a second time you'll have a revelation about how to solve it. (We've all left a test and said, "Oh yeah! Now I know what the answer to number 5 was.") Skipping the problem and then going back to it might give you a chance to have this revelation *during* the test, when it's still useful.

Follow the Template

Many students think the written-response section of the Geometry GSE is the most difficult part of the exam. Later in the book, we will spend time practicing exactly how to approach these written-response questions, so that you'll be comfortable with them by the time test day comes. For now, you only need to remember this about answering a written-response question: Provide explanations!

To receive a high score on the written-response section, you will need to provide explanations for the material you present. If you aren't sure about your answer, make sure you explain any rules you used to make your calculations. You can receive a lot of partial credit on this section for providing sound explanations, even if you don't end up with the correct answer. Students who leave things blank because they aren't sure of the answer will cost themselves lots of points on this section. The reverse is also true: Students may give a correct answer but still lose points for not providing a complete explanation. This is one area in which showing your work is not only helpful, it is vital to scoring well.

We will discuss strategies for the written-response questions in greater detail as we move through the review of geometry concepts.

YOU ARE IN CONTROL

We know that taking the Geometry GSE can be a stressful process. With all this built-up pressure, it might feel like this test is totally out of your control. But, the opposite is true—you are in control. Although you can't decide what number pencil (you must bring a #2) to bring to the exam or where to sit during the test, you can decide how you take the GSE. So let's review what we've discussed in this chapter:

- First, you must take advantage of the multiple-choice format of Part I. There is no guessing penalty, and you can use Process of Elimination to add points to your score, even without knowing the correct answer.

- Second, you can answer the multiple-choice questions in any order you want. Spend time with questions that you're comfortable with. If question 12 is really stumping you, move on to question 13, and return to 12 later.

- Third, you can gain points on the written-response section by providing clear explanations. Sometimes, mentioning a definition or rule can help you gain additional points, even if you do not know the correct answer.

As you build upon your knowledge of geometry by reviewing the chapters ahead, you'll gain more confidence in your ability to handle the exam.

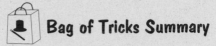 **Bag of Tricks Summary**

Here is a list of the tricks you'll find in that bag of yours—be sure to make good use of them.

- An Empty Scantron Sheet is a Bad Scantron Sheet.

- Use Process of Elimination (POE).

- So, I'll Just Start With #1 and Finish With #30, Right?

- The Two-Pass System.

- Follow the Template.

LINES AND ANGLES

THE BASICS

Geometry is the study of lines, angles, figures, planes, and solids. Even if you've never formally studied geometry before, no doubt you already have a wealth of knowledge on the subject gained through everyday experiences. You probably know, for example, that the shortest distance between two points is a straight line. You've also probably noticed that the closer you get to a building, the larger it appears. How about objects in a mirror that appear backwards? These geometric relationships, and others, will be explained in the chapters to follow.

When Euclid set up his system of geometry, he used definitions and postulates to prove his theorems. A postulate is considered to be a self-evident truth, one that cannot be proven. Theorems are conclusions that are logically derived from the postulates, with help from the definitions. In our review of geometry, we will not concern ourselves with these distinctions, except in the chapter on proofs. It's more important to know *how to use* a given theorem than it is to know whether it's a postulate or a theorem.

Definition of a Point

A **point** indicates a position in space, but has no dimensions (length, width, or height).

A point is most often represented by a dot on a page, or by a set of coordinates.

Point A can be represented as: . A or $A\ (5,3)$

Definition of a Line

A **line** has length, but no width or height.

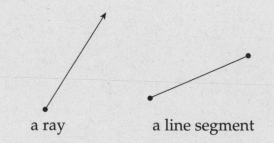

For any two points, there is exactly one line that intersects them. This means that if you know two points on a line, you can figure out which line is being referred to, because there is only one line that contains the two points. Lines extend indefinitely in opposite directions. The two main subsets of lines are **rays**, which start at one point, and extend indefinitely in one direction, and **line segments**, which have a specific length.

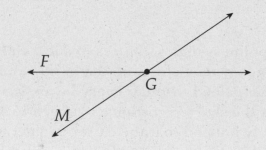

a ray   a line segment

The intersection of two nonidentical lines is a point. Line F and Line M intersect at point G.

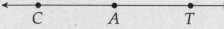

Every line segment has exactly one midpoint. The midpoint divides a line segment into two equal parts. Point A is the midpoint of line segment CT.

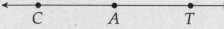

Definition of a Plane

Any flat surface is a plane. A chalkboard, the floor, and a tabletop are all examples of planes. For any three nonidentical and noncollinear (not lying on the same line) points, there is exactly one plane that intersects them. Planes extend forever in all directions. The intersection of two nonidentical planes is a line.

DEFINITION of an ANGLE

An **angle** is the measure between two rays that begin at the same point, and extend in different directions.

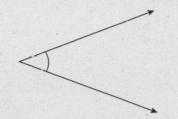

Angles are measured in degrees, and their measurements range from 0° to 360°. Angles with the measure of 90° are called **right angles**, angles less than 90° are **acute angles**, and angles greater than 90° are **obtuse angles**.

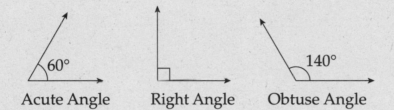

60°		140°
Acute Angle	Right Angle	Obtuse Angle

Complementary angles and **supplementary angles** are special relationships concerning right angles and straight lines. When two angles add up to 90°, they are said to be **complementary**, and when two angles add up to 180°, they are **supplementary**.

∠A and ∠B are complementary angles

∠C and ∠D are supplementary angles

An **angle bisector** is a ray that divides an angle into two congruent angles. If two angles are congruent and supplementary, they are right angles.

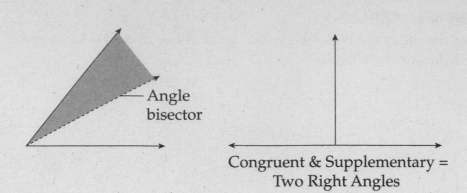

Angle
bisector

Congruent & Supplementary =
Two Right Angles

When two lines cross each other, they create two sets of congruent angles, called **vertical angles**. In the diagram below, $\angle 1 \cong \angle 3$ and $\angle 2 \cong \angle 4$.

There are a number of angle relationships formed when two parallel lines (lines that never intersect) are cut by a third line, called a **transversal**.

If two parallel lines are cut by a transversal, then:

• Corresponding angles are congruent:

- Alternate interior angles are congruent:

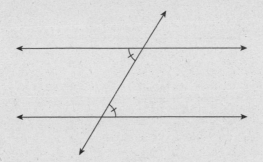

- Interior angles on the same side of the transversal are supplementary:

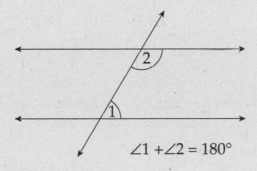

$$\angle 1 + \angle 2 = 180°$$

EXAMPLE 1

Lines *l* and *m* are parallel and cut by transversal *t*. What is the measurement of angle *X*? (see below)

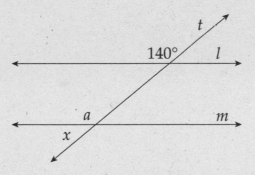

Here's How to Crack It

First, by applying the rule that states "corresponding angles are congruent," we know that m $\angle A = 140°$.

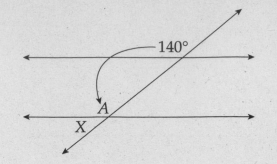

Next, by using our knowledge of supplementary angles, we notice that angles A and X are supplementary, and the sum of their measures must equal 180°. So, we can set up the following equation to solve for X.

$$m\angle X + 140° = 180°$$

$$m\angle X = 40°$$

The three theorems about parallel lines can also be used to prove that two lines are parallel. If two lines are cut by a transversal, and any of the following three statements are true, then the lines are parallel:

1. Corresponding angles are congruent.

2. Alternate interior angles are congruent.

3. Interior angles on the same side of the transversal are supplementary.

INTRODUCTION TO PROOFS

THE BASICS

In the process of completing a proof, you'll need to demonstrate that certain line segments and angles are **congruent** (the same size and shape). Congruency is denoted by the symbol "≅". The following rules of manipulation should be familiar from algebra, and you'll find that they are useful in completing proofs.

The first three rules can be memorized as the "RST" rules.

Property	Rule	Example
Reflexive	**Anything is equal (or congruent) to itself.**	$\angle A \cong \angle A$.
Symmetric	**You can always switch the order of the elements on either side of the "=" or "≅".**	If $\angle A \cong \angle B$, then $\angle B \cong \angle A$.
Transitive	**Two things that are equal/congruent to a separate third thing are equal/congruent to each other.**	If $\angle A \cong \angle B$ and $\angle B \cong \angle C$, then $\angle A \cong \angle C$.

You should also know these properties of equality, which can be applied to numbers, measures of angles, and lengths of line segments:

Addition Property of Equality: If $a = b$, and $c = \partial$, then $a + c = b + \partial$.

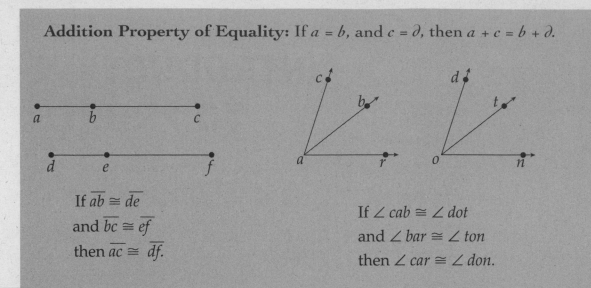

If $\overline{ab} \cong \overline{de}$
and $\overline{bc} \cong \overline{ef}$
then $\overline{ac} \cong \overline{df}$.

If $\angle cab \cong \angle dot$
and $\angle bar \cong \angle ton$
then $\angle car \cong \angle don$.

Subtraction Property of Equality: If $a = b$, and $c = \partial$, then $a - c = b - \partial$.

Multiplication Property of Equality: If k is a constant, and $a = b$, then $ka = kb$.

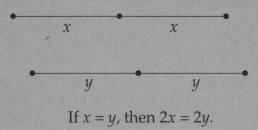

If $x = y$, then $2x = 2y$.

Substitution Property of Equality: If two quantities are equal, then one may be substituted for the other at any time.

Now that we have reviewed a number of rules that you'll need to solve proofs, let's turn to our first postulate, and our first proof. You should have two goals in mind while reviewing proofs: First, to learn the concepts of proofs; and second, to be able to use the various postulates and theorems in nonproof questions.

Segment Addition Postulate: If points A, B, and C are colinear, and point B is between points A and C, then $\overline{AB} + \overline{BC} = \overline{AC}$, and $\overline{AC} - \overline{AB} = \overline{BC}$, and $\overline{AC} - \overline{BC} = \overline{AB}$.

EXAMPLE 1

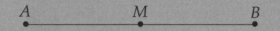

$$G \quad A \qquad\qquad M \quad E$$

Given: $\overline{GM} = \overline{AE}$ Prove: $\overline{GA} = \overline{ME}$

Here's How to Crack It

Statements	Reasons
1. $\overline{GM} = \overline{AE}$	1. Given
2. $\overline{AM} = \overline{AM}$	2. Reflexive Property of Equality
3. $\overline{GM} - \overline{AM} = \overline{AE} - \overline{AM}$	3. Subtraction Property of Equality
4. $\overline{GA} = \overline{ME}$	4. Segment Addition Postulate

> **Midpoint Theorem: The midpoint of a line segment divides it into two equal segments, each half as long as the original segment.**
>
>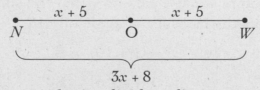
>
> If M is the midpoint of $\overline{AB}$, then $\overline{AM} \cong \overline{MB}$ and $\overline{AM} = \overline{MB} = \frac{1}{2}(\overline{AB})$.

EXAMPLE 2

O is the midpoint of line segment $\overline{NW}$. The length of $\overline{NW}$ is $3x + 8$, and the length of $\overline{NO}$ is $x + 5$. How long is $\overline{NW}$?

Here's How to Crack It

Since O is the midpoint of $\overline{NW}$, then $NO = OW$.

$$\overset{\displaystyle x+5}{\underset{N}{\rule{0pt}{0pt}}} \qquad \overset{\displaystyle x+5}{\underset{O}{\rule{0pt}{0pt}}} \qquad \underset{W}{\rule{0pt}{0pt}}$$

$$3x + 8$$

Since you know that a midpoint divides a line segment into two equal segments, you can set up your equation like this:

$$2(x + 5) = 3x + 8$$

$$2x + 10 = 3x + 8$$

$$2 = x$$

Now, plug in the value for x to solve for the length of NW.

$$3x + 8$$

$$3(2) + 8$$

$$14$$

The length of NW is 14.

Angle Addition Postulate: **If a ray *BD* lies in the interior of $\angle ABC$, then:**

$$\mathrm{m}\angle ABD + \mathrm{m}\angle DBC = \mathrm{m}\angle ABC$$

$$\mathrm{m}\angle ABC - \mathrm{m}\angle DBC = \mathrm{m}\angle ABD$$

$$\mathrm{m}\angle ABC - \mathrm{m}\angle ABD = \mathrm{m}\angle DBC$$

EXAMPLE 3

$\mathrm{m}\angle FAR = 80°$. If point T is in the interior of $\angle FAR$, and $\mathrm{m}\angle FAT = (6y - 7)°$, and $\mathrm{m}\angle TAR = (y + 10)°$, what is the value of y?

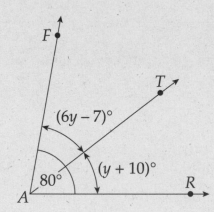

Here's How to Crack It

By using the angle addition postulate, we know that the sum of the measures of angles FAT and TAR equals the measure of angle of FAR.

$$(6y - 7)° + (y + 10)° = 80°$$

$$(7y + 3)° = 80°$$

$$7y° = 77°$$

$$y = 11$$

EXAMPLE 4

Prove that vertical angles are congruent.

Here's How to Crack It

The first thing you should do is draw a diagram. It's easier to organize your strategy with a visual effect.

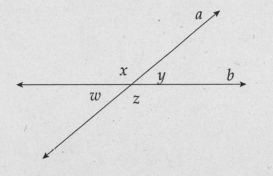

For this proof, it doesn't matter what the measures of the angles are, since we want to prove that vertical angles are **always** congruent, no matter what the measures of the angles are. So, to set up our proof, first we need to figure out what we have been given and what we want to prove.

GIVEN: $\angle x$ and $\angle z$ are vertical angles.

PROVE: $\angle x \cong \angle z$

Statements	Reasons
1. $\angle x$ and $\angle z$ are vertical angles	1. Given
2. $m\angle x + m\angle w = 180°$	2. Definition of supplementary angles
3. $m\angle x = 180° - m\angle w$	3. Subtraction Property of Equality (2)
4. $m\angle z + m\angle w = 180°$	4. Definition of supplementary angles
5. $m\angle z = 180° - m\angle w$	5. Subtraction Property of Equality (4)
6. $m\angle x = m\angle z$	6. Transitive Property (3,5)
7. $\angle x \cong \angle z$	7. Definition of Congruent Angles (6)

INTRODUCTION TO TRIANGLES

THE BASICS

Triangles are closed planar figures with three sides and three angles. The angles of a triangle always add up to 180°. The three types of triangles are right triangles, obtuse triangles, and acute triangles. **Right triangles** have one angle that is a right angle, **obtuse triangles** have one angle that is obtuse (greater than 90°), and **acute triangles** have three angles that are acute (less than 90°).

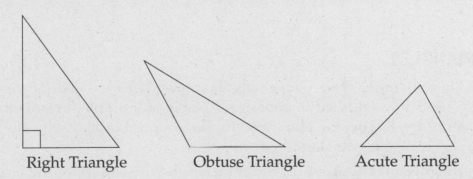

Right Triangle   Obtuse Triangle   Acute Triangle

There are three other categories of triangles: equilateral, isosceles, and scalene. **Equilateral triangles** have three congruent sides and three congruent angles, **isosceles triangles** have two congruent sides and two congruent angles, and **scalene triangles** have three unique sides and three unique angles.

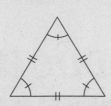
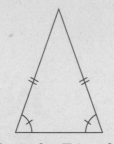
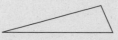

equilateral triangle
(each angle is 60°)

Isosceles Triangle
(angles opposite congruent
sides are congruent)

Scalene Triangle

The **altitude** (or height) of a triangle is a line segment drawn from one vertex perpendicular to the opposite side, or to the extension of the opposite side if the triangle is obtuse.

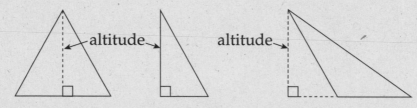

The **median** of a triangle is a line segment drawn from one vertex to the midpoint of the opposite side.

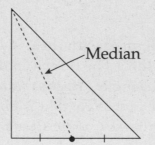

RIGHT TRIANGLES

You probably remember from your math class that there are many properties of right triangles that are studied in geometry. The most notable formula is—you guessed it—the **Pythagorean Theorem**. If you are not familiar with the Pythagorean Theorem, you should be.

The Pythagorean Theorem: In a right triangle, the square of the length of the hypotenuse is equal to the sum of the squares of the legs.

$$a^2 + b^2 = c^2$$

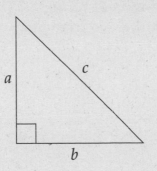

A common right triangle is the **3:4:5** triangle. Multiples of 3:4:5 are also right triangles.

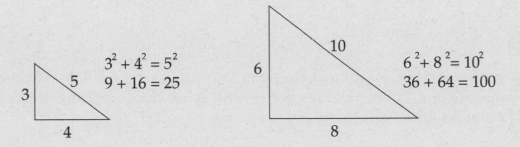

$$3^2 + 4^2 = 5^2$$
$$9 + 16 = 25$$

$$6^2 + 8^2 = 10^2$$
$$36 + 64 = 100$$

Other sets of Pythagorean triplets are **5:12:13, 8:15:17,** and **7:24:25**. Like 3:4:5 triangles, the multiples of these triplets are also right triangles. Most right triangles, however, will have at least one side that is not a rational number (it will be the square root of a number). There are two special right triangles that are formed by dividing a square or an equilateral triangle in half.

Half of a Square

As we all know, the sides of a square are congruent. Imagine drawing a line between two corners of a square.

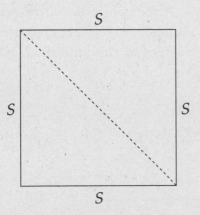

The result would be two congruent triangles. (In fact, you can fold the square along this line to illustrate that the two triangles are congruent.)

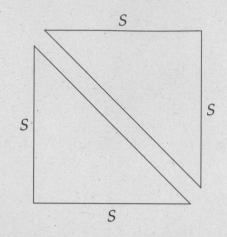

You will remember from the definition of an equilateral triangle that the two angles opposite congruent sides are congruent. Also, since we know that every triangle contains 180°, we can solve for the measure of the angles.

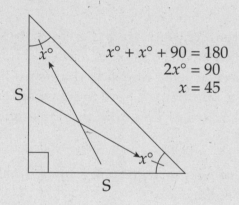

$$x° + x° + 90 = 180$$
$$2x° = 90$$
$$x = 45$$

This special triangle is sometimes called a **45° Right Triangle**. Looking back, it makes sense that the two angles are 45°, because the hypotenuse of the triangle bisected, or cut in half, the corners of the square. Finally, let's solve for the length of the hypotenuse.

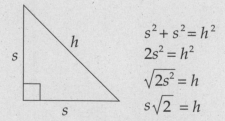

$$s^2 + s^2 = h^2$$
$$2s^2 = h^2$$
$$\sqrt{2s^2} = h$$
$$s\sqrt{2} = h$$

So, for any right triangle with two 45° angles, the hypotenuse will equal the length of a leg multiplied by the square root of 2.

Half of an Equilateral Triangle

As we've learned already, an equilateral triangle has three congruent sides and three congruent angles of 60° apiece. Equilateral triangles are unique in that their medians and altitudes are identical.

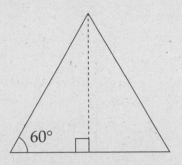

The two new triangles formed by the median are called 30-60-90 triangles, because those are the angles of the new triangle. Remember that the median bisects the side, creating two equal line segments. So, we now know that one leg is half the length of the hypotenuse. We can figure out the length of the third side by once again using the Pythagorean Theorem.

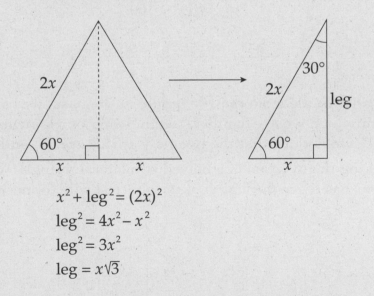

$$x^2 + \text{leg}^2 = (2x)^2$$
$$\text{leg}^2 = 4x^2 - x^2$$
$$\text{leg}^2 = 3x^2$$
$$\text{leg} = x\sqrt{3}$$

So, for all 30-60-90 triangles, the hypotenuse is twice the length of the side opposite the 30° angle, and the side opposite the 60° angle equals the length of the side opposite the 30° angle multiplied by the square root of 3.

EXAMPLE 1

In the diagram below, $LC = 100$. What is the length of TL?

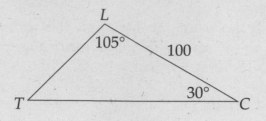

Here's How to Crack It

First, you should find the missing angle by remembering that the sum of the angles of a triangle equals 180°. So,

$$m\angle LTC + 105 + 30 = 180$$

$$m\angle LTC = 45$$

Next, the angles 30° and 45° should be familiar from special right triangles. However, there isn't a right angle in this triangle. How can that information help us?

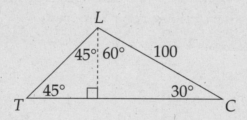

By drawing an altitude from the 105° angle to the base, we can create two right angles with which we are familiar. Again, using our knowledge that every triangle has 180°, we deduce that the two new angles are 45° and 60°.

By remembering the diagram of a halved equilateral triangle, we remember that the hypotenuse is twice the length of the shortest side (opposite the 30° angle).

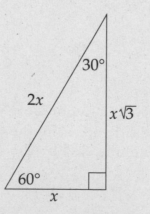

So, the altitude of the original triangle is 50, because it is half of 100. This leads us to the 45° right triangle. If the length of one leg is 50, then the other is too, because the two legs of a 45° right triangle are congruent. Lastly, by remembering that the hypotenuse of a 45° right triangle is the length of the side multiplied by the square root of 2, we come to our answer of:

$$50\sqrt{2}$$

We can double check using the Pythagorean theorem:

$$50^2 + 50^2 = c^2$$

$$2 \times 50^2 = c^2$$

$$50\sqrt{2} = c$$

Note: In chapter 6, you will learn the Law of Sines, which will give you an easier method to solve problems like this one.

EXAMPLE 2

Given: $\triangle MAN$ is equilateral. Prove: $AM = FM$.

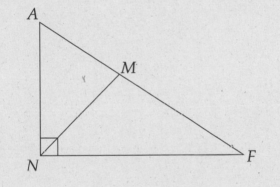

Here's How to Crack It

Statements	Reasons
1. $\triangle MAN$ is equilateral	1. Given
2. m$\angle MNA = 60°$	2. Definition of an equilateral triangle
3. m$\angle FNA -$ m$\angle MNA =$ m$\angle FNM$	3. Angle Addition Postulate
4. $90° - 60° =$ m$\angle FNM$	4. Substitution Principle
5. $30° =$ m$\angle FNM$	5. Substitution Principle
6. m$\angle AMN +$ m$\angle NMF = 180°$	6. Definition of Supplementary Angles
7. m$\angle AMN = 60°$	7. Definition of an equilateral triangle
8. $60° +$ m$\angle NMF = 180°$	8. Substitution Principle
9. m$\angle NMF = 120°$	9. Subtraction Property of Equality

10. m $\angle NFM$ + m $\angle FNM$ + m $\angle NMF = 180°$	10. Definition of a triangle
11. m $\angle NFM$ + 30° + 120° = 180°	11. Substitution Property
12. m $\angle NFM$ = 30°	12. Subtraction Property of Equality
13. $\triangle NMF$ is an isosceles triangle	13. Triangles with two $\cong$ angles are isosceles.
14. $MN = FM$	14. Definition of an isosceles triangle
15. $MN = AM$	15. Definition of an equilateral triangle
16. $AM = FM$	16. Transitive Property (14, 15)

SIMILAR TRIANGLES

Similar triangles are those which have three congruent angles, but are a different size. Since we can figure out the third angle of a triangle when we know the measures of two of its angles, if two angles of a triangle are congruent to two corresponding angles of a second triangle, then the two triangles are similar triangles. When two triangles are similar, we use the symbol "~" to represent this relationship. Below, triangle BOY ~ triangle MAN.

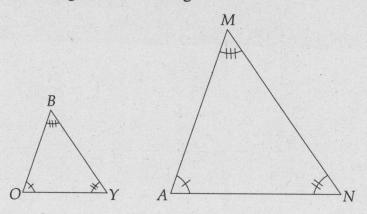

Another common diagram involving similar triangles looks like this, in which the triangles share an angle, and the bases are parallel:

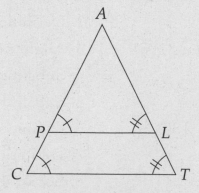

$\triangle CAT \sim \triangle PAL$

EXAMPLE 3

In the diagram below, line a is parallel to line b. Solve for x.

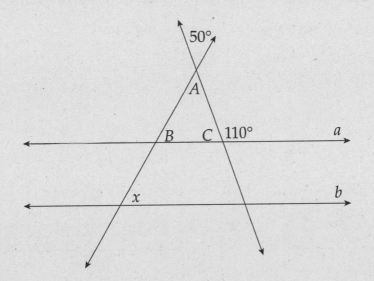

Here's How to Crack It

1. Label $\angle A$ as 50° because vertical angles are congruent.

2. Label $\angle C$ as 70° because supplementary angles sum to 180°. (180 − 110 = 70)

3. Label $\angle B$ as 60° because the angles in a triangle sum to 180°. (180 − 50 − 70 = 60)

4. Label $\angle x$ as 60° because corresponding angles are congruent. ($\angle B$ corresponds to $\angle x$.)

   ANSWER: $x = 60°$

Another way to solve this problem is to notice that $\angle B$ and $\angle X$ are corresponding angles of similar triangles, and thus congruent.

CONGRUENT TRIANGLES

Congruent triangles are similar triangles that are the same size. They have three congruent corresponding sides and three congruent corresponding angles.

Triangle *ABC* and triangle *LMN* are **congruent**:

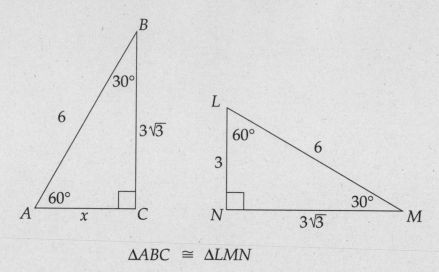

$$\triangle ABC \;\cong\; \triangle LMN$$

Although the triangles are rotated on the page, notice that the 60° angle is to the left of the right angle, and the 30° angle is to its right on both triangles. Angle *A* corresponds to angle *L*, line segment *AB* corresponds to line segment *LM*, and so on.

Triangle *ABL* and triangle *GHI* are **not congruent**:

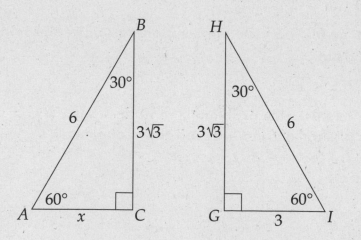

These two triangles are not congruent because the congruent sides and angles are not **corresponding** sides and angles. However, $\triangle ABC \cong \triangle IHG$. The order in which the letters are written *does* matter, as that is how we determine which sides and angles correspond to each other.

Although congruent triangles have three congruent corresponding sides and angles, it is possible for us to know that two triangles are congruent with less information. Here are the four theorems for determining congruency of triangles.

Side-Side-Side (SSS) Postulate: If three sides of a triangle are congruent to three corresponding sides of another triangle, then the triangles are congruent.

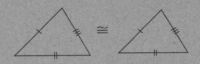

Side-Angle-Side (SAS) Postulate: If two sides and the included angle of one triangle are congruent to the corresponding parts of another triangle, then the triangles are congruent.

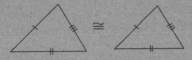

Angle-Side-Angle (ASA) Postulate: If two angles and one side of one triangle are congruent to the corresponding parts of another triangle, then the triangles are congruent.

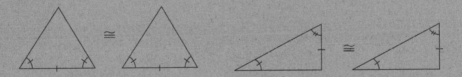

Notice that the side does not necessarily have to be the included side. This is because, technically, if we know two angles of a triangle, then we know the third, so, in this sense, all three sides are included sides.

Hypotenuse-Leg (HL) Postulate: If the hypotenuse and a leg of a right triangle are congruent to the corresponding parts of another right triangle, then the triangles are congruent.

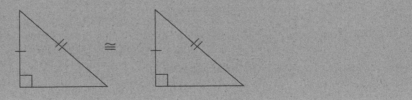

EXAMPLE 4

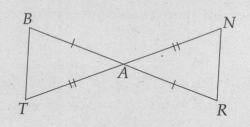

Given: Segments *TN* and *BR* bisect each other at point *A*.

Prove: $\triangle BAT \cong \triangle RAN$

Here's How to Crack It

Statements	Reasons
1. *TN* and *BR* bisect each other.	1. Given
2. $\overline{TA} \cong \overline{AN}$ and $\overline{BA} \cong \overline{AR}$	2. Definition of a bisector.
3. $\angle TAB \cong \angle RAN$	3. Vertical angles are congruent.
4. $\triangle BAT \cong \triangle RAN$	4. SAS $\cong$ SAS

Another rule that is often used in conjunction with the previous four postulates is the following:

> **CPCTC: Corresponding Parts of Congruent Triangles are Congruent.**

EXAMPLE 5

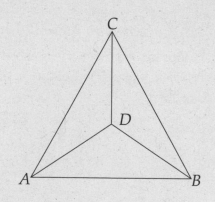

Given: $\angle DAB \cong \angle DBA$; $\angle ADC \cong \angle BDC$

Prove: $AC \cong BC$

Here's How to Crack It

Statements	Reasons
1. $\angle DAB \cong \angle DBA$	1. Given
2. $\triangle ADB$ is an isosceles triangle	2. Definition of an isosceles triangle
3. $\overline{AD} \cong \overline{DB}$ or $AD = DB$	3. Definition of an isosceles triangle
4. $\angle ADC \cong \angle BDC$	4. Given
5. $\overline{CD} \cong \overline{CD}$ or $CD = CD$	5. Reflexive Property
6. $\triangle ADC \cong \triangle BDC$	6. SAS $\cong$ SAS
7. $AC \cong BC$	7. CPCTC

AREA OF A TRIANGLE

The formula for the area of a triangle is:

$$A = 1/2\, bh$$

Area equals one half the base times the height.

In applying this formula, remember that the base is the length of a side, and the height is the altitude that connects that side with the opposite angle.

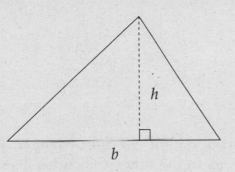

EXAMPLE 6

What is the area of $\triangle MLK$?

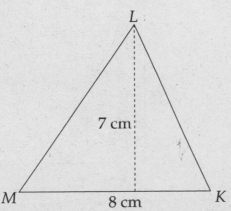

Here's How to Crack It

   1. We will use the formula for area of a triangle: $A = 1/2\,bh$

   2. Plug in the values for base and height: $A = 1/2\,(8 \times 7)$

   3. Perform the multiplication: $A = 28$

   4. Assign the correct units to the answer: $A = 28 \text{ cm}^2$

    NOTE: Remember that area is always given in **square units**.

EXAMPLE 7

The area of the triangle in the figure below is $18\sqrt{3}$ cm². What is the length of side a?

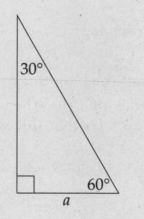

Here's How to Crack It

   1. Recognize that this is a 30-60-90 right triangle. With this information, we can assign values to the other two sides, based on the side we are solving for.

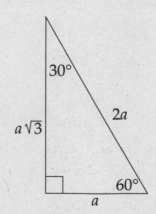

2. We now have a base and height for the triangle, and we can use the formula for area of a triangle to solve for a: $A = 1/2\ bh$

3. Plug in the quantities and variables: $18\sqrt{3}\ \text{cm}^2 = 1/2\ (a \times a\sqrt{3}\ )$

4. Divide both sides by 1/2 and $\sqrt{3}$: $36\ \text{cm}^2 = a^2$

5. Take the square root of each side: ANSWER: $a = 6\ \text{cm}$

QUADRILATERALS

THE BASICS

A **quadrilateral** is a closed polygon with four sides. The five types of quadrilaterals are: parallelogram, rhombus, rectangle, square, and trapezoid. Do you know the differences between all of them? If not, you should. Let's review.

PARALLELOGRAMS

A **parallelogram** is a quadrilateral whose opposite sides are parallel.

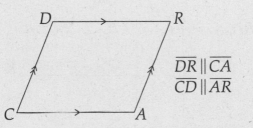

$$\overline{DR} \parallel \overline{CA}$$
$$\overline{CD} \parallel \overline{AR}$$

Characteristics of parallelograms:

- Opposite angles are congruent.

- Consecutive angles are supplementary.

- Opposite sides are congruent.

- Diagonals bisect each other.

EXAMPLE 1

In the parallelogram below, what is the measure of ∠ STU?

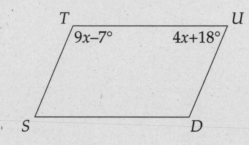

Here's How to Crack It

Since we know that consecutive angles of a parallelogram are supplementary (their sum equals 180°), we can set up an equation to solve for x.

$$(9x - 7) + (4x + 18) = 180$$

$$13x + 11 = 180$$

$$13x = 169$$

$$x = 13$$

Plug in the value for x: $9(13) - 7$

$$m\angle STU = 110°$$

EXAMPLE 2

Given: Parallelogram *RICK*. Prove: $\triangle RIC \cong \triangle CKR$

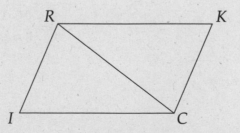

Here's How to Crack It

Statements	Reasons
1. *RICK* is a parallelogram	1. Given
2. $\overline{RC} \cong \overline{CK}$; $\overline{IC} \cong \overline{KR}$	2. Opposite sides of a parallelogram are congruent.
3. $\overline{RC} \cong \overline{RC}$	3. Reflexive Property
4. $\triangle RIC \cong \triangle CKR$	4. SSS $\cong$ SSS

This proof demonstrates that every parallelogram consists of two congruent triangles, which is a good way to explain the formula for area of a parallelogram.

Area of a Parallelogram

Remember the formula for the area of a triangle: $A = 1/2\ bh$

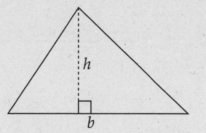

By making a parallelogram out of this triangle, the area is doubled:

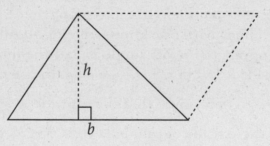

So, the formula for the area of a parallelogram is *double* the area of a triangle:

$$2 \times (\text{Area of a triangle})$$

$$2 \times (1/2\ bh)$$

$$\text{Area of a parallelogram} = bh$$

EXAMPLE 3

What is the area of the parallelogram below?

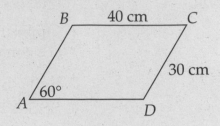

Here's How to Crack It

The formula for area of a parallelogram is base times height. (**A = bh**)

The base = 40 cm, but it is going to take a little work to come up with the height.

Notice that by drawing the altitude, we create a 30-60-90 right triangle:

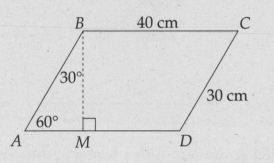

Since opposite sides of a parallelogram are congruent, then we know that the length of AB is 30 cm. Then, with our knowledge of 30-60-90 right triangles (namely, that the side opposite the 30° angle is half the length of the hypotenuse), we know that AM = 15 cm. Finally, we again use our knowledge about 30-60-90 right triangles to determine that the altitude = $15\sqrt{3}$.

Therefore, the area of the parallelogram is: $(40 \times 15\sqrt{3})$ cm², or $600\sqrt{3}$ cm².

RHOMBUSES

A **rhombus** is a special type of parallelogram, one with four congruent sides.

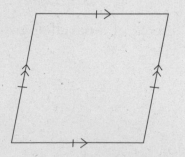

So, all the characteristics of parallelograms are also true of rhombuses:

- Opposite angles are congruent.

- Consecutive angles are supplementary.

- Opposite sides are congruent.

- Diagonals bisect each other.

In addition, rhombuses have these additional qualities, which set them apart from other parallelograms:

- Diagonals meet at right angles.

- Diagonals bisect the opposite angles.

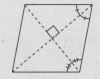

Area of a Rhombus

In addition to using the formula for parallelograms, there is a special formula that can be used for the area of rhombuses: $A = 1/2 \, (\partial_1 \times \partial_2)$, where ∂_1 and ∂_2 are the lengths of the two diagonals of the rhombus.

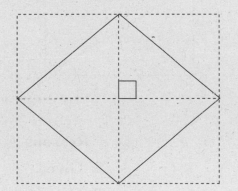

Notice that the rhombus takes up exactly half the area of in the rectangle in which it is circumscribed.

RECTANGLES

A **rectangle** is a special type of parallelogram, one with four right angles.

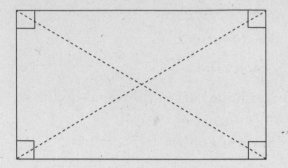

Rectangles have all the properties of a parallelogram, plus:

- Its diagonals are congruent.

- Each of its angles is a right angle.

EXAMPLE 4

Given: Rectangle *CARD*, diagonals *CR* and *AD* intersect at point *T*.
Prove: Δ *CTA* is an isosceles triangle.

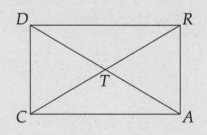

Here's How to Crack It

Statements	Reasons
1. *CARD* is a rectangle	1. Given
2. *CR* = *AD*	2. Diagonals of a rectangle are congruent
3. *CT* = 1/2 *CR*, and *TA* = 1/2 *AD*	3. Diagonals of a parallelogram bisect each other.
4. 1/2 *CR* = 1/2 *CR*	4. Reflexive Principle
5. 1/2 *CR* = 1/2 AD	5. Substitution Principle
6. *CT* = 1/2 *AD*	6. Substitution Principle
7. *CT* = *TA*	7. Substitution Principle
8. Δ *CTA* is an isosceles triangle	8. Triangles with two congruent sides are isosceles.

Area of a Rectangle

The formula for the area of a rectangle is length times width. $A = lw$

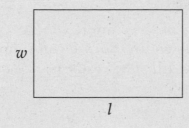

SQUARES

A **square** is a *very* special type of parallelogram. It has four congruent sides *and* four right angles.

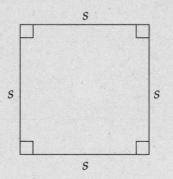

Since a square is both a rhombus *and* a rectangle, it possesses all the special properties of both rhombuses and rectangles:

- Its diagonals meet at right angles.

- Its diagonals bisect the opposite angles.

- Its diagonals are congruent.

The diagonals divide a square into four congruent 45° right triangles.

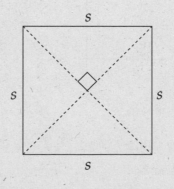

Area of a Square

Since a square is a type of rectangle and a type of rhombus, both of those formulas will work to calculate its area.

Using the formula for area of a rectangle ($A = lw$), notice that a square's length is *always* the same as its width. So, we can simplify the formula by substituting "side" for length and width. The result is: $A = s \times s$ or $A = s^2$.

EXAMPLE 5

In the figure below, what is the area of the shaded region?

Here's How to Crack It

1. Determine the area of the unshaded square. $A = s^2$

$$A = 5^2$$

$$A = 25 \text{ cm}^2$$

2. Draw in the diagonals of the unshaded square and use the Pythagorean theorem to discover the lengths.

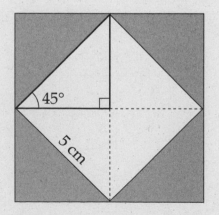

The diagonals form four congruent 45° Right Triangles, each with a hypotenuse of 5 cm. Label the legs of the triangle as x, and solve for x.

$$x^2 + x^2 = 5^2$$

$$2x^2 = 5^2$$

$$x^2 = 5^2/2$$

$$x = 5\sqrt{2}$$

So, the length of each diagonal of the unshaded square is $2(5/\sqrt{2}\,\text{cm})$ or $10/\sqrt{2}\,\text{cm}$. This is also the length of each side of the large square. So, using the formula for area of a square ($A = s^2$), we can derive the area of the large square.

$$A = (10/\sqrt{2})^2$$

$$A = 100/2$$

$$A = 50 \text{ cm}^2$$

Now, subtract the area of the unshaded square, and you will end up with the area of the shaded region.

$$50 \text{ cm}^2 - 25 \text{ cm}^2 = 25 \text{ cm}^2$$

So, the area of the shaded region is 25 cm².

TRAPEZOIDS

A **trapezoid** is a quadrilateral with exactly one pair of parallel sides.

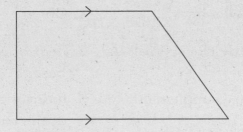

The parallel sides are called **bases**, and the nonparallel sides are called **legs**.

EXAMPLE 6

Given: Trapezoid *SILY* where *SI* and *LY* are parallel lines
Prove that ∠ *SIL* and ∠ *ILY* are supplementary.

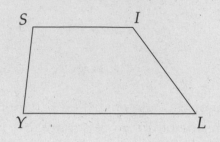

Here's How to Crack It

It may be easier to think about the trapezoid not as a shape, but as a group of intersecting lines.

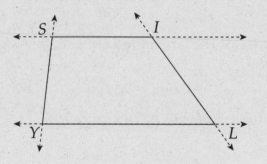

Statements	Reasons
1. $\overleftrightarrow{SI}$ and $\overleftrightarrow{LY}$ are parallel lines	1. Given
2. $\overleftrightarrow{SI}$ and $\overleftrightarrow{LY}$ are cut by transversal $\overleftrightarrow{IL}$	2. Legs of a trapezoid intersect the bases
3. ∠ *SIL* and ∠ *ILY* are supplementary	3. Interior angles on the same side of the transversal are supplementary.

An **Isosceles Trapezoid** is a trapezoid with two congruent legs.

EXAMPLE 7

Given: Trapezoid $TIFY$, $\overleftrightarrow{IF} \cong \overleftrightarrow{TY}$
Prove: $\angle IFY \cong \angle FYT$

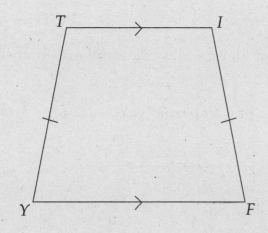

Here's How to Crack It
For this solution, we are going to use our knowledge of congruent triangles.

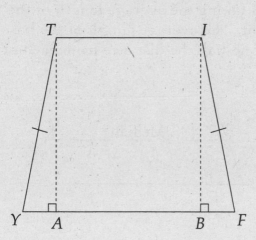

Statements	Reasons
1. $TIFY$ is a trapezoid	1. Given
2. $\overline{IF} \cong \overline{TY}$	2. Given
3. $\angle IBF$ and $\angle TAY$ are right angles	3. Definition of the height of a trapezoid
4. $\angle IBF \cong \angle TAY$	4. All right angles are congruent
5. TA is the height of trapezoid $TIFY$	5. Definition of the height of a trapezoid

6. *IB* is the height of trapezoid *TIFY*	6. Definition of the height of a trapezoid
7. $\overline{TA} \cong \overline{IB}$	7. Transitive Property
8. $\triangle IBF \cong \triangle TAY$	8. $HL \cong HL$
9. $\angle IFY \cong \angle FYT$	9. CPCTC

So, the **base angles** of an isosceles trapezoid are congruent.

Area of a Trapezoid

The formula for the area of a trapezoid is: $A = 1/2 \, (b_1 + b_2)h$

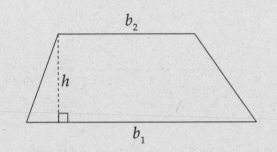

What we are doing is taking the average length of the two bases, and multiplying them by the height. The average length of the bases can be represented by a third parallel line, one-half the distance from each of the bases, called the **median**:

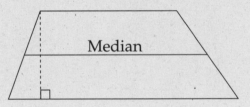

EXAMPLE 8

What is the area of the shaded region?

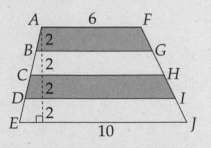

Here's How to Crack It

This problem is easier than it looks. Basically, you need to figure out the area of these two trapezoids:

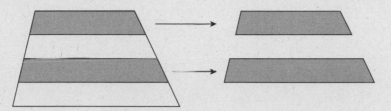

We know that line CH is the median of trapezoid $AFJE$ because it is equidistant from each of the bases. With this knowledge, we can figure out the length of CH.

$$\text{length of median} = 1/2 \ (b_1 + b_2)$$

$$CH = 1/2 \ (6 + 10)$$

$$CH = 8$$

By repeating this process, we can determine the lengths of lines BG and DI.

$BG = 1/2 \ (6 + 8)$	$DI = 1/2 \ (8 + 10)$
$BG = 7$	$DI = 9$

Now, we can use the formula for the area of a trapezoid to determine the areas of trapezoids $AFGB$ and $CHID$.

Area of $AFGB = 1/2 \ (b_1 + b_2)h$	Area of $CHID = 1/2 \ (b_1 + b_2)h$
Area of $AFGB = 1/2 \ (6 + 7) \times 2$	Area of $CHID = 1/2 \ (8 + 9) \times 2$
Area of $AFGB = 13$	Area of $CHID = 17$

Area of $AFGB + CHID = 30$ units^2

REGULAR POLYGONS

As you know, there are many other polygonal shapes other than parallelograms and trapezoids. For instance, the shape of a stop sign is a regular octagon. It has eight congruent sides and eight congruent angles. These congruencies are what make it "regular" and the fact that there are eight of them makes it an "octa"gon.

Some common regular polygons:

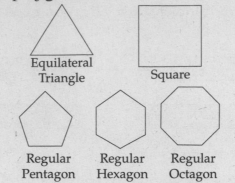

The formula for the *sum* of all angles in a polygon, whether or not it is a regular polygon, is:

$$180(n - 2)$$

So, *all* quadrilaterals (trapezoids, and all varieties of parallelograms) have a total of $180(4 - 2)°$, or $360°$.

The formula for the measure of the angle in a regular polygon with n sides is:

$$180(n - 2)/n$$

So, an equilateral triangle has three angles which measure $(180(3 - 2)/3)°$, or $60°$ each, and a regular pentagon has five angles which measure $(180(5 - 2)/5)°$, or $108°$ each.

These formulas provide you with an additional tool to help you crack those difficult questions on the Golden State Examination.

INTRODUCTION TO TRIGONOMETRY

THE BASICS

The trigonometry you need to know for the Geometry GSE relates almost exclusively to right triangles. You will remember from chapter 3 that every right triangle has two legs (a and b) and a hypotenuse (c).

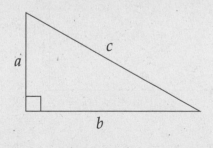

TRIGONOMETRIC RATIOS

Look at these three similar right triangles:

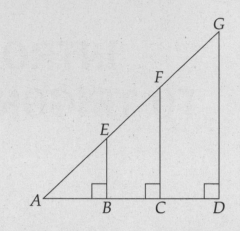

Since the triangles are similar, we know that their sides are proportional to each other. With this knowledge, we can create ratios that we know are equal to each other:

$$\frac{BE}{AE} = \frac{CF}{AF} = \frac{DG}{AG}$$

In other words, the ratio of the length of the side *opposite* $\angle A$ to the length of the *hypotenuse* is consistent. This ratio is known as the **sine** ratio (abbreviated as "sin").

$$\sin \angle A = \frac{\text{opposite}}{\text{hypotenuse}}$$

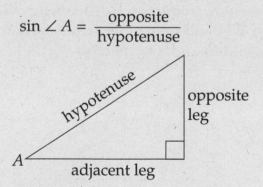

There are two other ratios that are used with right triangles: **cosine** (abbreviated as "cos"), and **tangent** (abbreviated as "tan"). Their ratios are:

$$\cos \angle A = \frac{\text{adjacent}}{\text{hypotenuse}}$$

$$\tan \angle A = \frac{\text{opposite}}{\text{adjacent}}$$

 The easiest way to memorize these ratios (and you should memorize them), is with the pneumonic device **SOHCAHTOA**:
Sine equals Opposite over Hypotenuse; Cosine equals Adjacent over Hypotenuse; Tangent equals Opposite over Adjacent.

EXAMPLE 1

Find the cosine of $\angle B$.

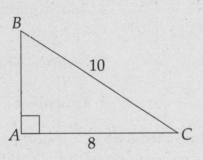

Here's How to Crack It

Although you do not know the length of the adjacent side, you recognize that $\triangle ABC$ is a 3:4:5 right triangle, which means that the adjacent side to $\angle B$ is 6. With this knowledge, we can employ the formula for cosine of an angle.

$$\cos \angle B = \frac{\text{adjacent}}{\text{hypotenuse}} = \frac{6}{10} = .6$$

EXAMPLE 2

Given: $\triangle SUN$; $\angle S$ is a right angle
Prove: $\sin \angle U = \cos \angle N$

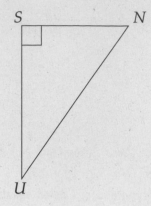

Here's How to Crack It

Statements	Reasons
1. $\triangle SUN$; $\angle S$ is a right angle	1. Given
2. $\sin \angle U = \dfrac{SN}{UN}$	2. sine = opposite over hypotenuse
3. $\cos \angle N = \dfrac{SN}{UN}$	3. cosine = adjacent over hypotenuse
4. $\sin \angle U = \cos \angle N$	4. Transitive Principle (3,4)

Furthermore, with the knowledge that $\angle U$ and $\angle N$ are complementary (their sum equals 90°), we can come up with the following equation:

$$\sin \angle X = \cos (90° - m\angle X) \quad \text{or} \quad \sin \theta = \cos (90 - \theta)$$

(The Greek letters ϕ (Phi) and θ (Theta) are often used to represent angles.)

EXAMPLE 3

Laura Anne plans to hike Half Dome, and she wants to know the grade of the trail so she can figure out how long it will take to complete the hike. She knows that the elevation at the base of the trail is 4,400 feet and the elevation at the peak is 8,800 feet. She also knows that the trail is 8.5 miles long. What is the average angle of elevation of the trail?

Here's How to Crack It

Although the angle of elevation of the trail changes dramatically at times, since we are looking for the **average** angle of elevation, we can draw a triangle that represents the average angle of elevation. The hypotenuse of the triangle will be 44,880 feet (8.5 × 5,280) and the height of the triangle will be 4,400 feet (8,800 − 4,400).

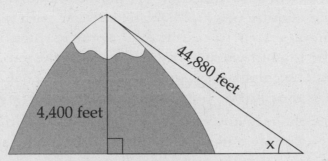

Since the angle we are looking for is angle x, and we have the lengths of the hypotenuse and side opposite to that angle, we are going to use the sine of x to solve for x.

$$\sin x = 4{,}400/44{,}880$$

$$\sin x = .0980$$

$$x = 5.624°$$

(For this step, you have to take the inverse of sine on your calculator. See "Using Your Calculator.")

SPECIAL TRIANGLES

At this point, it will be useful to note the trigonometric ratios of two triangles that you should be rather familiar by now: the 30-60-90 triangle, and the 45° right triangle. However, as long as you can figure out the lengths of the sides (it may be helpful to remember that a 30-60-90 triangle is half of an equilateral triangle, and that a 45° right triangle is half of a square), and you know how to use the Pythagorean theorem and SOHCAHTOA, you can figure out these ratios by yourself:

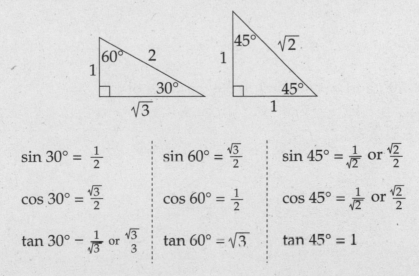

$$\sin 30° = \tfrac{1}{2} \qquad \sin 60° = \tfrac{\sqrt{3}}{2} \qquad \sin 45° = \tfrac{1}{\sqrt{2}} \text{ or } \tfrac{\sqrt{2}}{2}$$

$$\cos 30° = \tfrac{\sqrt{3}}{2} \qquad \cos 60° = \tfrac{1}{2} \qquad \cos 45° = \tfrac{1}{\sqrt{2}} \text{ or } \tfrac{\sqrt{2}}{2}$$

$$\tan 30° - \tfrac{1}{\sqrt{3}} \text{ or } \tfrac{\sqrt{3}}{3} \qquad \tan 60° = \sqrt{3} \qquad \tan 45° = 1$$

USING YOUR CALCULATOR

Calculators with trigonometry functions are permitted during the Geometry GSE, so you should acquire one and become familiar with it before the test. Here are some general instructions, but refer to the calculator's manual for instructions specific to your calculator. First of all, make sure that the calculator is in **degree mode**. The calculator is in degree mode if "DEG" appears on the display. If not, press the "DRG" button until "DEG" appears.

When you know the measure of an angle, and you would like to generate its trigonometric ratios, simply enter the measure of the angle, and then press the ratio you would like to generate, "sin," "cos," or "tan."

When you know a trigonometric ratio and you would like to generate the measure of the angle, simply enter the value of the ratio, then press the second function button (usually labeled "2ND" or "INV"). Then press the button that corresponds to the ratio that you entered. (If you entered the cosine ratio for the angle in question, then you will press "cos" at this time.) This process is called taking the "inverse" of sine, cosine, and tangent.

Law of Sines

This is a rule that holds true for *all* triangles, not just right triangles. The Law of Sines states: In any triangle, the ratio of the sine of an angle to the length of the opposite side is constant for that triangle.

$$\text{Or: } \sin A/a \ = \ \sin B/b \ = \ \sin C/c$$

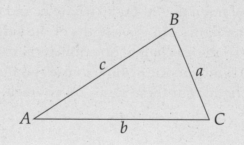

EXAMPLE 4

If $A = 40°$, $B = 30°$, and $a = 4$, what is the measure of b?

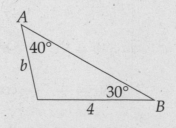

Here's How to Crack It

Using the Law of Sines, we get: sin 40°/4 = sin 30°/b

$$.6428/4 = .5/b$$

$$b \approx 3.1114$$

CAUTION: There are cases when the Law of Sines equation could be true for two different triangles. These are always cases when you are given two sides and a nonincluded angle.

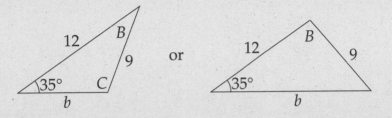

You will notice that the measures of angles B and C and the measure of side b are different in the two figures above. This is called the *Ambiguous Case*, which means that there are two possible correct answers.

The ambiguous case only occurs when the following two conditions are satisfied:

1. You are given two sides and a nonincluded angle.

2. When given sides a and b, and angle A, then $b \sin A < b < a$.

If we tried to solve for C in the diagram above, we would get:

$$\sin 35°/9 = \sin C/12$$

$$\sin C = .7648$$

$$C \approx 50°$$

(This answer obviously applies to the triangle on the right, because C is obtuse in the left triangle.)

However, when we check the conditions of the ambiguous case:

1. You are given two sides and a nonincluded angle. ✔

2. 12 sin 35 < 9 < 12 ✔ (12 sin 35 ≈ 6.883)

In these cases, the correct measurement of angle C in the left triangle is 180 minus the measurement that was given after taking the inverse of sine (50). So, the measurement of angle C in the left triangle is 180 − 50, or 130°.

CIRCLES

THE BASICS

A **circle** is a locus (a set) of points that are equidistant to a common point, which is called the **center**. A circle contains 360 degrees.

Imagine an infinite number of congruent line segments, all starting at the same point, and extending into all different directions.

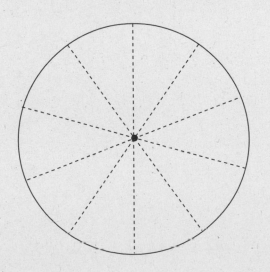

Together, the endpoints of all the line segments form a circle. Another way to imagine this concept is to picture a piece of string attached to a chalkboard with a nail, and a piece of string is tied to the other end. If you held the chalk so the string was taut, you could draw a perfect circle.

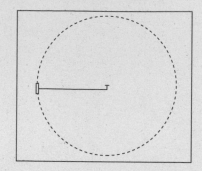

This is the same concept that was used to design the compass (The kind used in geometry, not the kind used to tell direction!).

The distance from the center of a circle to any point on the circle is called the **radius**.

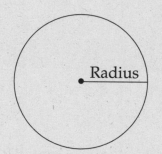

A **secant** is a line that passes through any two points on a circle.

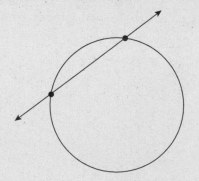

A **chord** is a line segment whose two endpoints are on a circle.

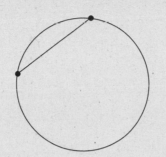

A **diameter** is a special kind of chord. It passes through the center, and it is the longest chord in a circle.

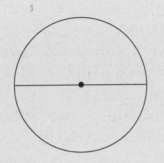

Since the diameter passes through the center of a circle, its length is twice the length of the radius of the same circle.

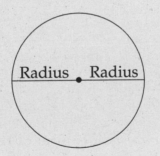

diameter = 2 × radius

A **tangent** is a line that passes through only one point on a circle.

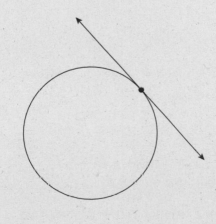

The radius, which contains the point of tangency, forms a right angle with the tangent.

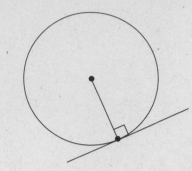

ARCS

An **arc** is a portion of a circle, and it is measured in degrees. Questions on the Golden State Examination may require you to determine the measure of an arc based on its relationships with various angles. This section will give you the tools you need to solve such problems.

A **semicircle** is an arc that measures exactly 180°. It is half of a circle (semi means half). A diameter subtends a semicircle.

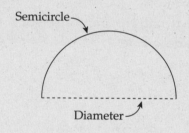

Semicircle

Diameter

CENTRAL ANGLES

A **central angle** is formed by two radii (plural of radius). This means that the vertex of the angle is the center of the circle (hence the name "central" angle). A central angle has the same measure as the arc it **subtends**.

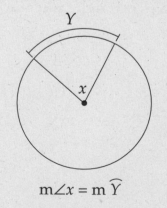

Y

x

$$m\angle x = m\,\widehat{Y}$$

EXAMPLE 1

In the figure, the circle with center C has a diameter US, and radius CD. If the measure of $\angle UCD$ is 70°, what is the measure of arc SD?

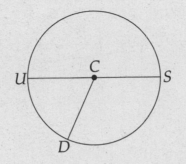

Here's How to Crack It

Remember from the definition of a diameter that it is a line segment. Also, notice that $\angle UCD$ and $\angle SCD$ are supplementary angles (they add up to 180°). So, if the measure of $\angle UCD$ is 70°, then the measure of its supplementary angle ($\angle SCD$) is $(180 - 70)$°, or 110°. Lastly, recognize that $\angle SCD$ is a central angle and it subtends arc SD. So, since the measure of a central angle is the same as the measure of the arc that it subtends, the measure of arc SD is 110°.

INSCRIBED ANGLES

An **inscribed angle** is formed by two chords. This means that the vertex of the angle is a point on the circle. An inscribed angle has half the measure of the arc it subtends.

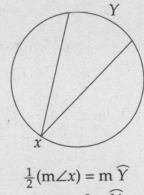

$$\tfrac{1}{2}(m\angle x) = m\,\widehat{Y}$$
$$m\angle x = 2m\,\widehat{Y}$$

EXAMPLE 2

In the figure, what is the measure of X?

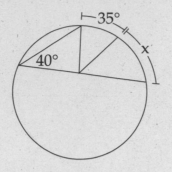

Here's How to Crack it

The measure of the angle subtended by the inscribed angle is twice the measure of the angle, therefore it is $2 \times 40°$, or $80°$. After subtracting that $35°$ angle, we find that the measure of X is $45°$ ($80° - 35°$).

When two chords intersect **inside** a circle, the measure of the angles formed is the average of their subtended arcs.

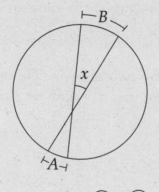

$$m\angle x = \tfrac{1}{2}(m\widehat{A} + m\widehat{B})$$

EXAMPLE 3

In the figure below, m$\angle MRY = 30°$, m$\angle YAT = 25°$. What is the measure of $\angle AYR$?

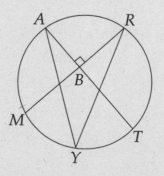

Here's How to Crack It

The solution of this problem takes quite a few steps, but as long as you keep your concepts about angles in a circle straight, it shouldn't be too difficult.

$\angle MRY$ and $\angle YAT$ are inscribed angles, so the arcs that they subtend will have a measure that is twice the measure of their respective angles, so:

$$\text{arc } MY = 2 \times 30° = \textbf{60°} \quad \text{and} \quad \text{arc } YT = 2 \times 25° = \textbf{50°}$$

Using the information that $\angle ABR = 90°$, we can solve for the measure of arc AR, because we know that the average of the measures of arc MT and AR is the same as the measure of $\angle ABR$, which is 90°. The measure of arc MT is the sum of the measures of arc MY and arc YT, or 110°.

$$m\angle ABR = 1/2 \, (m\overset{\frown}{MT} + m\overset{\frown}{AR})$$
$$90° = 1/2 \, (110° + m\overset{\frown}{AR})$$
$$90° = 55° + 1/2 \, (m\overset{\frown}{AR})$$
$$35° = 1/2 \, (m\overset{\frown}{AR})$$
$$70° = m\overset{\frown}{AR}$$

Now that we know that $\overset{\frown}{AR} = 70°$, we can solve for the measure of $\angle AYR$.

$$m\angle AYR = 1/2 \, (m\overset{\frown}{AR})$$
$$m\angle AYR = 1/2 \, (70°)$$
$$m\angle AYR = 35°$$

ANGLES OUTSIDE A CIRCLE

The next type of angles we need to be concerned with are those that lie outside the circle, and whose legs are either two secants, two tangents, or a secant and a tangent.

In these cases, the measure of the angle is equal to half the difference between the major arc and the minor arc.

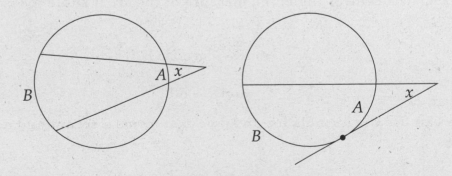

In both cases,
$$x = \tfrac{1}{2}(m\overset{\frown}{B} - m\overset{\frown}{A})$$

EXAMPLE 4

In the figure below, secant CZ passes through center R and point A on the circle. Line ZY is tangent to the circle at point Y. The measure of $\angle CZY = 30°$. What are the measures of arc AY and arc CY?

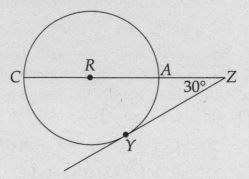

Here's How to Crack It

To solve for AY, we will need to remember that the radius RY forms right angle $\angle RYZ$.

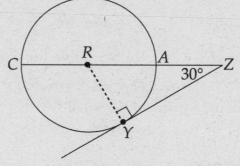

Using our knowledge of triangles, we can solve for $\angle ZRY$.

$$m\angle ZRY = 180° - m\angle RYZ - m\angle RZY$$

$$m\angle ZRY = 180° - 30° - 90°$$

$$m\angle ZRY = 60°$$

Since $\angle ZRY$ is a central angle, the measure of the arc it subtends is equal to its measure.

$$m\stackrel{\frown}{AY} = m\angle ZRY$$

$$m\stackrel{\frown}{AY} = 60°$$

Now, we can use the formula for an angle that forms a secant and a tangent with a circle:

$$m\angle RZY = 1/2\ (m\stackrel{\frown}{CY} - m\stackrel{\frown}{AY})$$

$$30° = 1/2\ (m\stackrel{\frown}{CY} - 60°)$$

$$30° = 1/2 \ (m\overset{\frown}{CY}) - 1/2 \ (60°)$$

$$30° = 1/2 \ (m\overset{\frown}{CY}) - 30°$$

$$60° = 1/2 \ (m\overset{\frown}{CY})$$

$$120° = m\overset{\frown}{CY}$$

As a check on our work, notice that $\angle CRY$ is a central angle that subtends $\overset{\frown}{CY}$, so its measure is also 120°. Next, notice that $\angle CRY$ and $\angle ARY$ are supplementary angles, so their sum should equal 180°, and it does:

$$120° + 60° = 180°$$

As we already know, the angle formed at the point where a diameter (or radius) meets a tangent is a right angle. The more general rule, which applies to any chord, is: The measure of an angle formed by a tangent and a chord is equal to half of the measure of its intercepted arc.

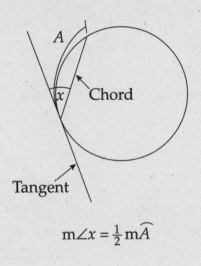

$$m\angle x = \tfrac{1}{2} \, m\overset{\frown}{A}$$

Two tangents drawn from the same point are congruent.

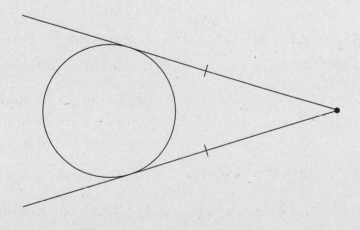

EXAMPLE 5

Given: A circle has tangents $\overline{AC}$ and $\overline{AD}$.

Prove: $m\overset{\frown}{CD}$ (minor arc) $= 180 - m\angle A$

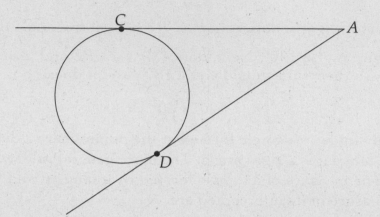

Here's How to Crack It

Statements	Reasons
1. $\overline{AC}$ and $\overline{AD}$ are tangents of a circle	1. Given
2. Construct chord $\overline{CD}$	2. Possible construction
3. $\overline{AC} \cong \overline{AD}$	3. Two tangents from the same point are congruent.
4. $\triangle ACD$ is an isosceles triangle	4. Triangles with two congruent sides are isosceles triangles.
5. $m\angle D = m\angle C$	5. Angles opposite congruent sides of a triangle are congruent.
6. $m\angle A + m\angle C + m\angle D = 180°$	6. The angles of a triangle sum to 180°
7. $m\angle A + m\angle C + m\angle C = 180°$	7. Substitution Principle
8. $m\angle C = 1/2 \, (180° - m\angle A)$	8. Algebraic Simplification
9. $m\angle C = 1/2 \, (m\overset{\frown}{CD})$	9. The angle formed by a tangent and a chord equals half the measure of its intercepted arc.
10. $1/2 \, (m\overset{\frown}{CD}) = 1/2 \, (180° - m\angle A)$	10. Transitive Principle
11. $m\overset{\frown}{CD}$ (minor arc) $= 180 - m\angle A$	11. Algebraic Simplification

So, we now have another tool in determining the measures of angles and arcs. The minor arc that is subtended by two tangents equals 180° minus the measure of the angle formed where the two tangents intersect. (This rule obviously does not apply to parallel lines since they do not intersect. However, the arc subtended by two tangential parallel lines is 180°.)

From this rule, we can derive the equation for the measure of the major arc, since we know that a circle contains 360°.

$$360° - (180° - m\angle A)$$

$$180° + m\angle A$$

So, the major arc that is subtended by two tangents equals 180° plus the measure of the angle formed where the two tangents intersect.

For each chord, there is exactly one diameter (or radius) which intersects the chord at a right angle. This diameter (or radius) bisects the chord into two equal segments.

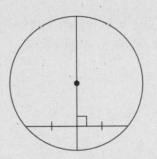

If two chords intersect within a circle, then the product of the lengths of the segments of one chord is equal to the product of the lengths of the other.

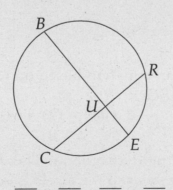

$$\overline{BU} \times \overline{UE} = \overline{CU} \times \overline{UR}$$

Given a point exterior to a circle, the square of the tangent segment to the circle is equal to the product of the lengths of the secant and its external segment.

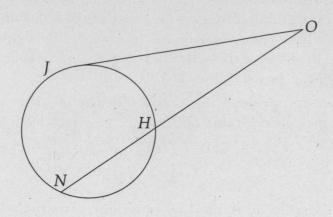

$$JO^2 = ON \times OH$$

EXAMPLE 6

In the figure, *BC* is tangent to the circle, and secant *CE* forms a right angle with chord *BD*. What are the values of *x*, *y*, and *z*?

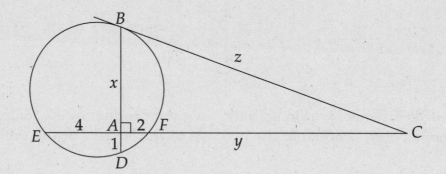

Here's How to Crack It

To solve for *x*, we will set up an equation based on the equality of the products of the parts of chords *BD* and *EF*.

$$1 \bullet (x) = (2) \bullet (4)$$
$$x = 8$$

To solve for *y*, we will use the Pythagorean Theorem, and the rule that states, "The square of the tangent segment to the circle is equal to the product of the lengths of the secant and its external segment."

Pythagorean Theorem:

$$8^2 + (y + 2)^2 = z^2$$
$$y^2 + 4y + 68 = z^2$$

Tangent/secant rule:

$$y \bullet (y + 6) = z^2$$

$$y^2 + 6y = z^2$$

Use the Transitive Property:

$$y^2 + 6y = y^2 + 4y + 68$$

$$y = 34$$

To solve for y, we could use either the Pythagorean Theorem, or the tangent/secant rule. In this example, I will use the tangent/secant rule.

$$y \bullet (y + 6) = z^2$$

$$34 \bullet (34 + 6) = z^2$$

$$z = \sqrt{1360} \approx 36.8782$$

TANGENTIAL RELATIONSHIPS BETWEEN CIRCLES

Circles may be tangent to each other and there are two ways that this can happen: internally and externally.

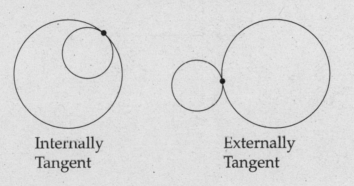

Internally Tangent

Externally Tangent

Two circles may also be tangent to the same line in two fashions. If the circles are on the same side of the line, it is a **common external tangent**. If the circles are on opposite sides of the line, it is a **common internal tangent**.

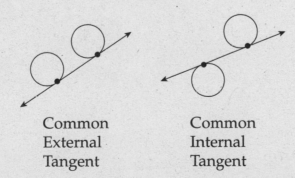

Common External Tangent

Common Internal Tangent

A line that passes through the centers of two circles is called the **line of centers**.

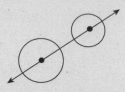

When two circles are tangent to each other, either internally or externally, the line that is tangent to both circles is perpendicular to the line of centers.

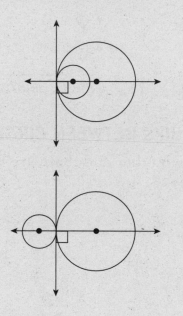

PROPERTIES OF THREE-DIMENSIONAL FIGURES

REVIEW OF TWO-DIMENSIONAL PROPERTIES

Two-dimensional objects are those which have length and width, and exist on a plane. Parallelograms, triangles, circles, and trapezoids are all examples of two-dimensional objects. The two properties we're concerned with are perimeter, which is the sum of the lengths of the lines that make up a shape, and area, which we've already covered for triangles and quadrilaterals.

Perimeter

For triangles, just add up the lengths of the sides to calculate the perimeter.

For squares and rhombuses, the perimeter is $4s$ (where s is the length of one side).

For parallelograms and rectangles, the perimeter is $2l + 2w$ (where l is the length, and w is the width, or length of the shorter sides).

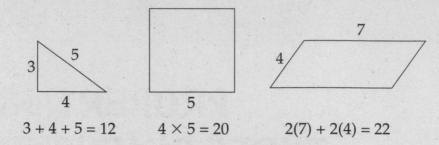

| $3 + 4 + 5 = 12$ | $4 \times 5 = 20$ | $2(7) + 2(4) = 22$ |

The perimeter of a circle is called the **circumference**. It is calculated using the irrational number π (pi). If your calculator doesn't have a π button, pi can be estimated as 3.14.

$$\text{circumference} = \text{pi times diameter}$$

$$c = \pi\partial$$

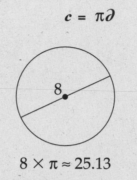

$$8 \times \pi \approx 25.13$$

It is also possible to calculate the length of an arc (although this is rarely tested on the GSE). The formula for the length of an arc is based on the formula for the circumference of a circle, but a factor is multiplied in to account for the proportion of the circle represented by the arc.

$$\text{arc length} = (ca/360)\,\pi\partial \text{ (where } ca \text{ is the measure of the central angle)}$$

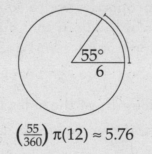

$$\left(\frac{55}{360}\right)\pi(12) \approx 5.76$$

AREA

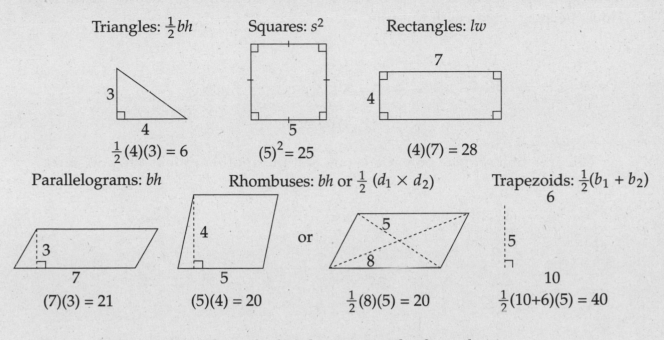

Triangles: $\frac{1}{2}bh$

$\frac{1}{2}(4)(3) = 6$

Squares: s^2

$(5)^2 = 25$

Rectangles: lw

$(4)(7) = 28$

Parallelograms: bh

$(7)(3) = 21$

Rhombuses: bh or $\frac{1}{2}(d_1 \times d_2)$

$(5)(4) = 20$ or $\frac{1}{2}(8)(5) = 20$

Trapezoids: $\frac{1}{2}(b_1 + b_2)$

$\frac{1}{2}(10+6)(5) = 40$

The area of a circle is also calculated using pi. The formula is:

$$A = \pi r^2 \quad \text{(where r is the length of the radius)}$$

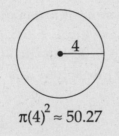

$\pi(4)^2 \approx 50.27$

   A **sector** is a portion of a circle (a slice of the pie). The formula for the area of a sector is based on the formula for the area of a circle, but a factor is multiplied in to account for the proportion of the circle represented by the sector.

$$A = (ca/360)\,\pi r^2 \quad \text{(where } ca \text{ is the measure of the central angle)}$$

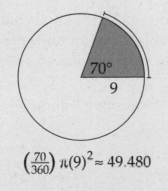

$\left(\frac{70}{360}\right)\pi(9)^2 \approx 49.480$

The area of regular polygons is calculated using a measurement called an **apothem**. The apothem of a polygon is the distance from the center to one of the sides, perpendicular with the side.

Apothem

The area of a regular polygon is one half the apothem times the perimeter.

$$A = 1/2 \ ap$$

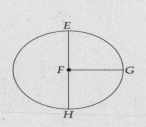

THE THIRD DIMENSION

Using these formulas for area, we can now calculate the first property of solids: **surface area**. Surface area is the sum of areas of all surfaces of a solid. For example, the surface area for a square cube is $6s^2$. The easiest way to calculate surface area most of the time is to imagine the solid "unfolded" onto a plane. This is what a square cube looks like when it is "unfolded."

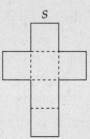

Volume is the amount of three-dimensional space that an object takes up. You may have measured the volume of an object in science class using a graduated cylinder. In geometry, we use formulas to calculate volume. (Big surprise, eh?)

For each of the following shapes, we'll show you how to calculate the surface area and volume.

Rectangular Boxes
Surface Area = $2lw + 2lh + 2wh$
Volume = lwh

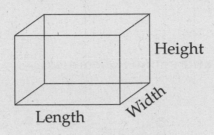

EXAMPLE 1
Calculate the surface area and volume for this refrigerator:

Here's How to Crack It
Surface Area = $2(3)(3) + 2(3)(6) + 2(3)(6)$ = 90 square units
Volume = $(3)(3)(6)$ = 54 cubic units

Cylinders
When 'unfolded', a cylinder is two circles and a rectangle. The circles are the top and bottom, and the rectangle is the side.

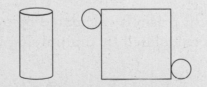

First, we calculate the area or the two circles, which is $2\pi r^2$. Next, we calculate the area of the rectangle, which is lw or bh. However, the length of the base of the rectangle happens to be the circumference of the circle, making it $\pi\partial h$.

So, the total surface area for a cylinder is $2\pi r^2 + \pi\partial h$.

The formula for the volume of a cylinder is the area of the base times the height, or:

$$V = \pi r^2 h$$

EXAMPLE 2

Calculate the surface area and volume of this can.

Here's How to Crack It

Surface Area = $2\pi(3)^2 + \pi(6)(7) \approx 188.5$ square units

Volume = $\pi(3)^2 7 \approx 197.92$ cubic units

Right Prisms

A *right prism* is a term for a polyhedron with two bases of polygons and sides in the shape of rectangles. The sides intersect the bases at right angles.

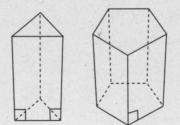

The surface area of a right prism is calculated by adding the area of the bases to the lateral area, which is calculated by multiplying the perimeter by the height.

$$SA = 2(1/2\ ap) + ph = p(a + h)$$

The volume is the area of the base times the height, or:

$$V = (1/2\ ap)h$$

EXAMPLE 3

Calculate the surface area and volume for a regular right hexahedron with height of 6, and the length of a base side equal to 4.

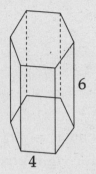

Here's How to Crack It

First, to calculate the area of the hexagon, we will need to determine the length of the apothem. Remember that the angles of a regular hexagon are $(180(6-2))/6°$ or $120°$. By bisecting each of the angles, we can create the following triangle:

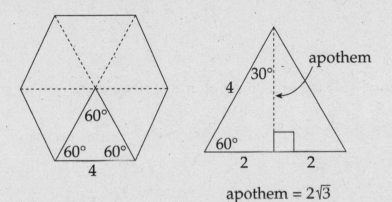

apothem = $2\sqrt{3}$

Now that we have the length of the apothem, we can substitute it into the equation for surface area:

$$SA = p(a + h)$$

$$SA = (6 \times 4)(2\sqrt{3} + 6) \approx 227.138 \text{ square units}$$

$$\text{Volume} = (1/2ap)h$$

$$\text{Volume} = (1/2)(2\sqrt{3})(6 \times 4)(6) \approx 249.415 \text{ cubic units}$$

Cones

A cone is a solid whose base is a circle, and whose top is a vertex. Here is what a cone looks like when it is "unfolded." (However, this is one case when it will be easier just to memorize the formula.)

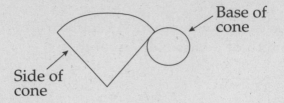

Base of cone

Side of cone

The area of the circle at the base is: πr^2

The area of the lateral surface is: $\pi r s$ (s = slant—the distance along the side of the cone, from vertex to base)

Combined, we get **total surface area** = **$\pi r(r + s)$**

Note: this formula works only for **right circular cones**, which are the regular cones you should be familiar with. In a right circular cone, the height forms a right angle with the radius at the center of the base.

Volume is simpler: one-third the area of the base times the height. This will be the same for pyramids. Since the base of a cone is a circle, the formula pans out as:

$$V = 1/3 \ \pi r^2 h$$

EXAMPLE 4

Calculate the total surface area and volume of this right circular cone.

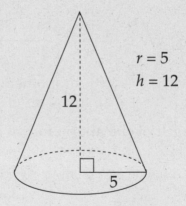

$r = 5$

$h = 12$

12

5

Here's How to Crack It

The formula for surface area is $\pi r(r + s)$. However, the question did not give us the length of the slant. We can figure out the length of the slant by noticing that the radius, height, and slant form this right triangle:

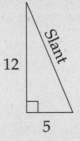

Now, we can easily use the Pythagorean theorem to solve for the length of the slant:

$$5^2 + 12^2 = s^2$$

$$s = 13$$

Now we can employ the formula for surface area:

$$SA = \pi r(r + s)$$

$$SA = \pi 5(5 + 13)$$

$$SA \approx 282.7 \text{ square units}$$

$$\text{Volume} = 1/3 \, (\pi 5^2)12 \approx 314 \text{ cubic units}$$

Pyramids

Pyramids are similar to cones in that they have a base and a vertex, but the base of a pyramid is in the shape of a polygon. Also, the sides are in the shape of congruent isosceles triangles.

"Unfolded", a pyramid with a square base looks like this:

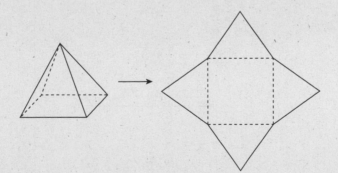

To calculate the surface area, you first calculate the area of the base a^2 (a = length of base side), and then calculate the area of the sides. Each side has an area of $1/2 \, bh$. On a pyramid, the slant height (s) is used to calculate surface area of the side. Combined, the formula for surface area of a square pyramid is:

$$SA = a^2 + 4 \, (1/2 \, as)$$

The volume is similar to a cone: $1/3\ bh$. Since the base of a pyramid is a square, the area of the base is a^2. So, here is the formula for the volume of a pyramid:

$$V = 1/3\ a^2h$$

EXAMPLE 5

Calculate the surface area and volume for this equilateral pyramid with a square base, with the length of one side of the base = 6.

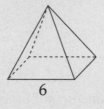

Here's How to Crack It

First, calculate the area of the base:

$$b = 6^2 = 36 \text{ square units}$$

Next, you will need to calculate the area of the sides. In order to do this, you will need to determine the slant height. Since the solid in question is a right equilateral pyramid, you know that each side is an equilateral triangle. Now, knowing that the length of the base of the side = 6, you can construct the following triangle:

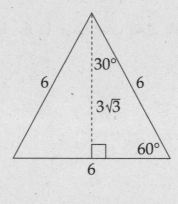

$$s = 3\sqrt{3}$$

$$SA = 6^2 + 4\ (1/2\ (6)(\ 3\sqrt{3})) \approx 98.3538 \text{ square units}$$

Next, to calculate the volume, we will need to determine the height of the pyramid. The easiest way to do this is to notice that the height, slant, and half the length of the base side make the following right triangle:

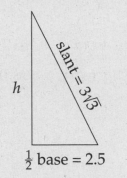

Using the Pythagorean Theorem, we can determine the height of the pyramid:

$$h^2 + (2.5)^2 = (3\sqrt{3})^2$$

$$h \approx 4.555$$

Now we can calculate the volume:

$$V \approx 1/3\ (6^2)(4.555) \approx 54.672 \text{ cubic units}$$

Spheres

When "unfolded," spheres make a very strange shape that is difficult to manipulate, so we won't bother unfolding the sphere. (In fact, the awkwardness of the unfolded shape is why a flat map has adjusted lines of latitude and longitude, elongating the shapes/sizes of some countries).

The formula for the surface area of a sphere is:

$$SA = 4\pi r^2$$

The formula for the volume of a sphere is:

$$V = 4/3\,(\pi r^3)$$

EXAMPLE 6

Calculate the surface area and volume of a sphere with a diameter of 8.

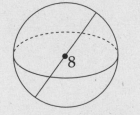

Here's How to Crack It

First, we will need to calculate the length of the radius, since it is not given to us.

$$r = 1/2 \partial$$

$$r = 4$$

$$\text{Surface Area} = 4\pi(4)^2 \approx 201.06 \text{ square units}$$

$$\text{Volume} = 4/3(\pi(4)^3) \approx 268.08 \text{ cubic units}$$

COORDINATE GEOMETRY

THE BASICS

Two-dimensional objects are mapped onto a grid called the Cartesian coordinate plane. The two axes (plural of axis) divide the plane into four quadrants.

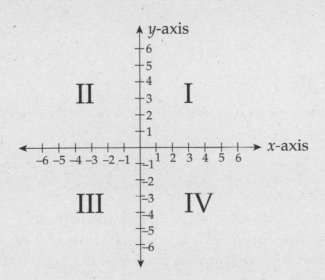

Each of the quadrants varies on the sign (positive or negative) of the x and y coordinates.

Here is a quick reference chart that tells you the sign of the x and y values.

Quadrant I: (+,+)

Quadrant II: (–,+)

Quadrant III: (–,–)

Quadrant IV: (+,–)

A point on the grid is assigned a set of **coordinates**, sometimes called **ordered pairs** (because the order matters). Ordered pairs are given in the form **(x,y)**, where x is the values along the x (horizontal) axis, and y is the value along the y (vertical) axis. The coordinates for the points in the graph below are: A(1,0); B(0,–3); C(2,2); D(–4,1)

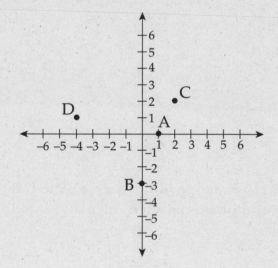

EQUATION OF A LINE

The equation for a line is given in the form: $y = mx + b$, where m is the slope, and b is the y-intercept.

> **Slope = rise over run.**

In other words, distance traveled along the y-axis divided by distance traveled along the x-axis. For instance, a line with a slope of 1 travels one unit up (positive on the y-axis) for every unit it travels to the right (positive on the x-axis).

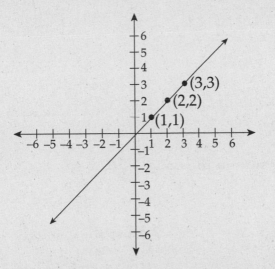

A horizontal line has a slope of zero, and a vertical line is said to have "no slope." In order to remember this easier, picture yourself skiing on a vertical or horizontal slope, and remember the phrase, *"No slope = no hope. Zero slope = zero fun."*

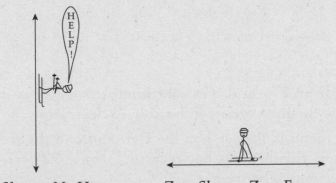

No Slope = No Hope   *Zero Slope = Zero Fun*

The **y-intercept** is the location where the line crosses the y-axis. If the equation of a line is $y = 3x + 2$, then we know that the slope of the line is 3, and it crosses the y-axis at $(0,2)$. This is because when you substitute zero for x, the equation simplifies to $y = 2$. This brings up an important point. If you know the equation for a line, you can determine whether or not a given point is on that line by substituting its coordinates into the equation for the line. If the sentence is still an equality, then the point is on the line.

EXAMPLE 1

Is (−2,4) on the line $y = 1/2\, x - 5$?

Here's How to Crack It
Substitute:

$$4 \stackrel{?}{=} 1/2\,(-2) - 5$$

$$4 \neq -6$$

Therefore, (−2,4) is not on the line $y = 1/2\, x - 5$.

EXAMPLE 2

At what point does the line $y = -2x + 7$ cross the x-axis?

Here's How to Crack It
This question can also be phrased as: "On this line, what is the x-coordinate when the y-coordinate equals zero?"

To solve this question, simply substitute zero for y, and solve for x.

$$0 = -2x + 7$$

$$x = 7/2 \text{ or } 3.5$$

So, the line $y = -2x + 7$ crosses the x-axis at: (3.5,0)

Measuring Distance

One of the most useful formulas in coordinate geometry is the **distance formula**. With the distance formula, you will be able to determine the distance of a line.

The distance formula is based on the Pythagorean theorem. For example, in the diagram below, the distance between (2,1) and (5,3) can be determined using the Pythagorean Theorem.

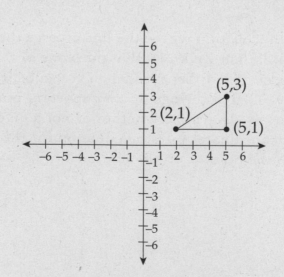

The square of the length of one side is: $(5 - 2)^2 = 9$.

The square of the other side is: $(3 - 1)^2 = 4$.

Therefore, the length of the hypotenuse is $\sqrt{(9 + 4)}$ or $\sqrt{13}$.

You may have noticed that we took the square of the difference of the x-coordinates, and added it to the square of the difference of the y-coordinates, and then took the square root of the sum. This process will give you the length of any line segment for which you know the coordinates of the endpoints, and can be simplified as follows:

For coordinates (x_1, y_1) and (x_2, y_2), the distance between them is:

$$\sqrt{(x_2 - x_1)^2 + (y_2 - y_1)^2}$$

EXAMPLE 3

What is the distance of the segment of the line ($y = 6x - 20$) that lies in quadrant IV?

Here's How to Crack It

First of all, you will need to remember that quadrant IV is the region where the x-coordinates are positive, and the y-coordinates are negative. (It's the lower right quadrant in a standard graph.) So, the question is asking what length of the line lies to the right of the y-axis and below the x-axis?

If we first determine the points where the line crosses the x- and y-axes, then we would have the endpoints of the line in question. First, substitute zero for x, and solve for y:

$$y = 6(0) - 20 = -20$$

So, our first endpoint is $(-20,0)$.

Now, substitute zero for y, and solve for x:

$$0 = 6x - 20$$

$$x = 20/6 = 10/3$$

So, our second endpoint is $(0,10/3)$

Now we can use the distance formula to determine the length of the line segment.

$$\partial = \sqrt{(-20 - 0)^2 + (0 - 10/3)^2}$$
$$\partial = \sqrt{400 + 100/9}$$

$$\partial \approx 20.2759 \text{ units}$$

Finding the Midpoint

The next important formula of coordinate geometry is the midpoint formula. To calculate the midpoint of a line segment, you take the average of its coordinates:

$$\text{midpoint} = ((x_1 + x_2)/2, (y_1 + y_2)/2)$$

EXAMPLE 4

What is the midpoint of the line segment that has $(-2,3)$ and $(17,-4)$ as its endpoints?

Here's How to Crack It
Simply substitute the values into the formula.

$$\text{midpoint} = ((-2 + 17)/2, (3 + -4)/2)$$

$$= (7.5, -.5)$$

EXAMPLE 5

If the midpoint of a segment is $(2,-3)$ and one of the endpoints of that segment is $(-3,-4)$, find the coordinates of the other endpoint.

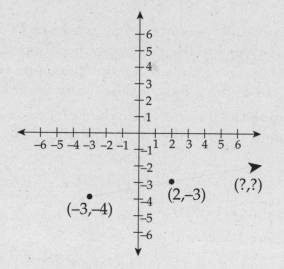

Here's How to Crack It
Use the midpoint formula to solve for the coordinates, one at a time.

$$\text{Midpoint } x = (x_1 + x_2)/2$$
$$2 = (-3 + x_2)/2$$
$$x_2 = 7$$
$$\text{Midpoint } y = (y_1 + y_2)/2$$
$$-3 = (-4 + y_2)/2$$
$$y_2 = -2$$

So, the coordinates of the other midpoint are: $(7,-2)$.

EQUATION OF A CIRCLE

The next formula is for the equation of a circle. In the following equation, (h,k) is the coordinates of the center of the circle, and r is the radius:

$$(x - h)^2 + (y - k)^2 = r^2$$

By manipulating this equation, you can determine at what point (or points) the circle crosses the x- or y-axis. Also, you can determine whether of not a point lies on a given circle or not.

EXAMPLE 6

At what point or points does the circle $(x + 2)^2 + (y - 5)^2 = 53$ cross the x-axis? What is the center and radius of this circle?

Here's How to Crack It
Determining where the circle crosses the x-axis is the easy part. Just substitute zero for y and solve for x:

$$(x + 2)^2 + (0 - 5)^2 = 53$$

$$(x + 2)^2 = 28$$

$$x = -2 \pm \left(\sqrt{28}\right) \approx 3.2915 \text{ or } -7.2915$$

So, the circle crosses the x-axis at: (3.2915, 0) **and** (–7.2915, 0)

Now, in order to determine the radius and the coordinates for the center of the circle, we need to make sure that the formula for the circle is in the proper form: $(x - h)^2 + (y - k)^2 = r^2$.

The given equation: $(x + 2)^2 + (y - 5)^2 = 53$

is the same as: $(x - (-2))^2 + (y - 5)^2 = \left(\sqrt{53}\right)^2$

except for the fact that the second equation is in a format that is more useful to us.

Now that our equation is in the proper form, it is easy to determine the radius:

$$r = \sqrt{53} \approx 7.28$$

Also, it is easy to determine the coordinates for the center:

$$\text{center} = (-2,5)$$

TRANSFORMATIONAL GEOMETRY

Transformational Geometry refers to the process of taking a set of points and changing it in some respect. The changed set of points is called the *image* of the original set of points. The main types of transformation are: **translations**, **reflections**, **rotations**, and **dilations**. Performing a transformation on an object is kind of like acting as a photocopy machine that changes the original object in a specific fashion (enlarging or decreasing its size, for example).

Translations

A translation refers to moving a point or set of points the same distance in the same direction. In a translation, the figure, size, and shape of the set of points does not change, only the location changes.

If a point $P(x,y)$ is translated a units horizontally and b units vertically, its image is $P'(x + a, y + b)$.

$$(x, y) \xrightarrow{\text{T}_{a,b}} (x + a, y + b)$$

EXAMPLE 7

Given points $A(2,3)$, $B(1,-2)$, and $C(-2,0)$, what is the graph of $\triangle ABC$ under $T_{4,-1}$?

A.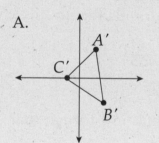

B.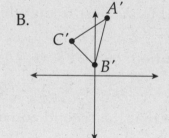

C.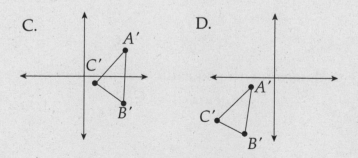

D.

Here's How to Crack It

Before freaking out about the lack of numbers on the graphs, take a look at them and see if you notice any major differences.

Each of the C' points are in characteristically different locations: the x-axis, Quadrant II, Quadrant IV, and Quadrant III. So, if you solve for C, you can shorten your time spent crunching numbers, and get on to the next problem.

$$C(-2, 0) \xrightarrow{T_{4,-1}} C'((-2+4), (0-1)) \text{ or } C'(2,-1)$$

Since the coordinates of C are $(2,-1)$, C lies in Quadrant IV.

ANSWER: C

As a double check, the values for A and B are:

$$A(2, 3) \xrightarrow{T_{4,-1}} A'((2+4), (3-1)) \text{ or } A'(6, 2)$$

$$B(1, -2) \xrightarrow{T_{4,-1}} B'((1+4), (-2-1)) \text{ or } B'(5, -3)$$

A is $(6,2)$ and thus in Quadrant I, and B is $(5,-3)$ and thus in Quadrant IV. Answer C checks out.

Reflections

A reflection refers to finding the mirror image of a point, where a given line acts as the mirror. Sets of points that are reflected do not change in size or shape, only in location and orientation.

If point $P(x,y)$ is reflected in the **y-axis**, its image is $p'(-x,y)$.

$$(x,y) \xrightarrow{R_{y=axis}} (-x,y)$$

The sign of the x coordinate changes, and the y coordinate remains the same.

If point $P(x,y)$ is reflected in the **x-axis**, its image is $p'(x,-y)$.

$$(x,y) \xrightarrow{R_{x\text{-}axis}} (x,-y)$$

The sign of the x coordinate remains the same, and the y coordinate changes.

If point $P(x,y)$ is reflected in the line $y = x$, its image is $p'(y,x)$.

$$(x,y) \xrightarrow{R_{y=x}} (y,x)$$

The x- and y-coordinates are interchanged.

EXAMPLE 8

The point $P(-3,4)$ has been reflected through the line $y = x$, and then reflected through the y-axis. What are the coordinates of P'?

      A. $(-4,-3)$ B. $(4,3)$ C. $(3,-4)$ D. $(-3,-4)$

Here's How to Crack It

The first thing to remember is to perform the reflections in the order stated. If you mix up the order, you will get an incorrect answer.

$$\text{Step 1} \quad (-3, 4) \xrightarrow{\text{R}_{y=x}} (4, -3)$$

$$\text{Step 2} \quad (4, -3) \xrightarrow{\text{R}_{y\text{-axis}}} (-4, -3)$$

ANSWER: A

Rotations

A rotation refers to moving a point or set of points around a given point. You will only need to worry about rotations around the origin $(0,0)$, so that is all we will deal with here. A rotation through a positive angle is counterclockwise, and a rotation through a negative angle is clockwise. Once again, only location and orientation are being changed, not size or shape.

If a point $P(x,y)$ is rotated $90°$, its image is $P'(-y,x)$.

$$(x,y) \xrightarrow{\text{Rot}_{90°}} (-y, x)$$

If a point $P(x,y)$ is rotated $180°$, its image is $P'(-x,-y)$.

$$(x,y) \xrightarrow{\text{Rot}_{180°}} (-x,-y)$$

If a point $P(x,y)$ is rotated $270°$ (or $-90°$), its image is $P'(y,-x)$.

$$(x, y) \xrightarrow{\text{Rot}_{270°}} (y, -x)$$

EXAMPLE 9

How many degrees is $(-4,3)$ rotated from $(4,-3)$?

      A. $90°$ B. $180°$ C. $270°$ D. $-90°$

Here's How to Crack It

First off, choices C and D are equivalent answers, which eliminates them both as possible answers. You should notice that both coordinated changes signs, but they didn't trade values. This means that it was a $180°$ rotation. However, in case you don't memorize these rules, you can always draw a graph to help you figure it out.

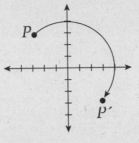

Considering that (0,0) is the center of the rotation, how many degrees is the arc in the figure? Out of the choices available, 180° is the only reasonable answer.

ANSWER: B

Dilations

A dilation refers to the stretching or shrinking of a set of points. The amount by which the points are stretched or shrunk is called a *scale factor*. In a dilation, the shape stays the same, but **size changes**, so the figure and its image are *similar*, but not *congruent*.

If point P(x,y) is dilated with a scale factor of k, its image is P' (kx,ky).

$$(x, y) \xrightarrow{\quad D_k \quad} (kx, ky)$$

EXAMPLE 10

If the circle $(x + 9)^2 + (y - 14)^2 = 29$ were dilated by a factor of .25, what would be the location of the dilated center?

A. (2.25,3.5)   B. (.25,.25)   C. (7.25,2.25)   D. (–2.25,3.5)

Here's How to Crack It

First off, the given equation needs to be converted into the proper form:

$$(x - (-9))^2 + (y - 14)^2 = \left(\sqrt{29}\right)^2$$

So, the original center of the circle is: (–9,14).

Now, perform the dilation:

$$(-9,14) \xrightarrow{\quad D_{.25} \quad} (-2.25,3.5)$$

ANSWER: D

PRACTICE TEST ONE

SAMPLE MULTIPLE-CHOICE QUESTIONS FOR GEOMETRY

Make sure you have two or three No. 2 pencils with erasers and a ruler or straightedge available to you during the exam. You also may have a calculator; it may be either a scientific or graphing calculator. You may not use minicomputers, pocket organizers, or calculators with QWERTY (typewriter) keyboards. You may not share your calculator with other students.

Do not spend too much time on a question that seems too difficult. Answer the easier questions first and then return to the harder ones if you have the time. Try to answer every question, even if you have to guess.

Notes: (1) Figures that accompany problems are drawn as accurately as possible EXCEPT when it is stated that a figure is not drawn to scale. All figures lie in a plane unless otherwise indicated.

(2) All numbers used are real numbers. All algebraic expressions represent real numbers unless otherwise indicated.

TEST ONE, DAY ONE

1. In the figure, $\angle \ell$ and $\angle m$ are supplementary, $\angle m$ and $\angle n$ are supplementary, $\angle n$ and $\angle o$ are complementary, and the measure of $\angle o$ is 36°. What is the measure of $\angle \ell$?

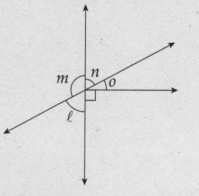

Note: Figure not drawn to scale.

A. 90°   B. 36°   C. 54°   D. 126°

2. In the figure, if line a and line b are parallel, what is the measurement of $\angle x$?

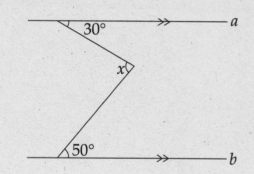

Note: Figure not drawn to scale.

A. 60°   B. 80°   C. 40°   D. 50°

3. There are three shapes in the figure: regular pentagon *ABCDH*, right triangle *HDG*, and square *DGEF*. What is the degree measure of ∠*CDE*?

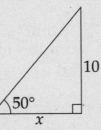

Note: Figure not drawn to scale.

A. 126°   B. 234°   C. 198°   D. 144°

4. In the triangle, what is the value of *x*?

Note: Figure not drawn to scale.

A. 10/(tan 50)

B. (tan 50)/10

C. 10 • tan 50

D. 1/(10 • tan 50)

5. In the figure, $\overline{AB}$ and $\overline{GE}$ are diameters of the circle *O*. What is the degree measure of arc *CD*?

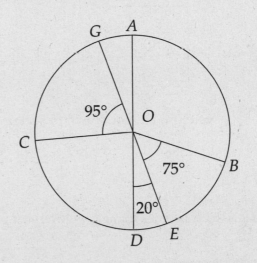

Note: Figure not drawn to scale.

A.   10   B. 65   C. 85   D. 30

6. In the figure, if the perimeter of the parallelogram is 120, and *EB* = 10, what is *AB*?

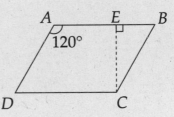

Note: Figure not drawn to scale.

A. 80   B. 40   C. 30   D. 12

7. What is the surface area of the cube in the figure?

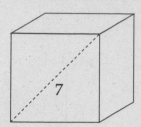

Note: Figure not drawn to scale.

A. 294   B. 588   C. 147   D. 49

8. What is the area of the triangle with vertices (–7,0), (–4,0), and (–5,5)?

A. 25 square units

B. 20 square units

C. 7.5 square units

D. 5.5 square units

9. What is the measure of ∠BAM?

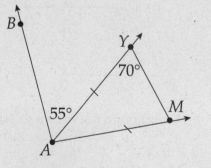

Note: Figure not drawn to scale.

A. 95°   B. 90°   C. 15°   D. 98°

10. What is the measure of ∠ABC to the nearest tenth?

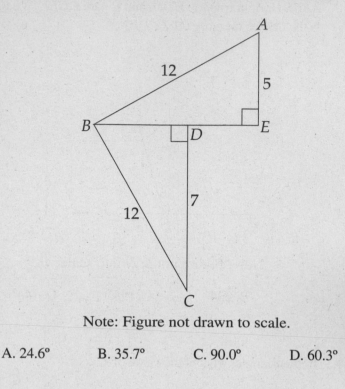

Note: Figure not drawn to scale.

A. 24.6°   B. 35.7°   C. 90.0°   D. 60.3°

11. In the figure, if $\overline{AC}$ and $\overline{BD}$ are diameters, $AC = 20$, and the measure of ∠AOD = 100°, what is the length of the arc AB?

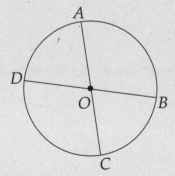

Note: Figure not drawn to scale.

A. $1,600\,\pi$

B. $4\dfrac{4}{9}\pi$

C. $90\,\pi$

D. $10\,\pi$

12. What is the surface area of a right circular cone with a diameter of 10 and a height of 15 (in square units)?

  A. 150

  B. 150π

  C. 104π

  D. $1,500\pi$

13. In the figure, $a - b =$

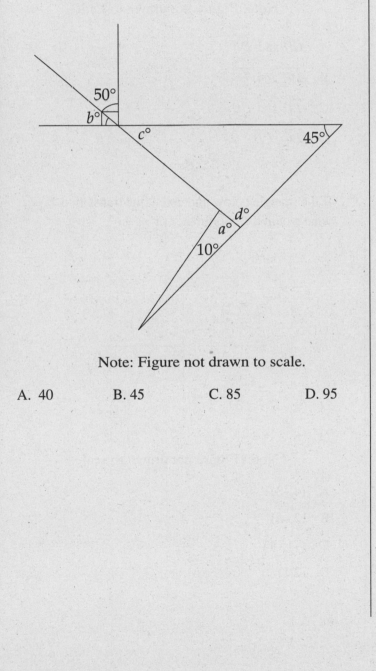

Note: Figure not drawn to scale.

A. 40   B. 45   C. 85   D. 95

14. A square is circumscribed within a circle with a radius of 4. What is the area of the shaded region (in square units)?

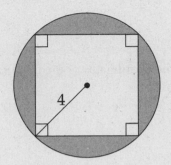

Note: Figure not drawn to scale.

  A. $16\pi^2$

  B. 16π

  C. $16\pi - 32$

  D. $16\pi + 32$

15. In the figure, ABC is an equilateral triangle. In addition, $\overline{BC}$ and $\overline{DE}$ are parallel. If $AE = 40$, what DE?

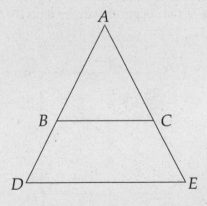

Note: Figure not drawn to scale.

  A. 40

  B. $40/\sqrt{3}$

  C. 20

  D. 60

16. If the measure of the largest angle of an isosceles triangle is 122° and its longest side is 40, what is the length of its other two sides to the nearest tenth?

A. 22.9　　　B. 17.5　　　C. 15.5　　　D. 34.2

17. What are the coordinates of the point (3,5) reflected by the *y*-axis?

  A. (–3,–5)

  B. (3,–5)

  C. (–3,5)

  D. (5,3)

18. If the volume of a right hexagonal prism is 3,444 cubic units, its height is 12 units, and the perimeter of the hexagonal base is 82 units, what is the length of its apothem?

A. 4　　　B. 24　　　C. 7　　　D. 32

19. In the figure, *ABF* and *ACE* are similar triangles. The length of $\overline{AB}$ is one-fourth the length of $\overline{AC}$. What is the area of the square (in square units)?

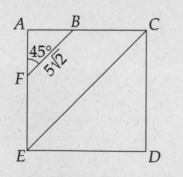

Note: Figure not drawn to scale.

A. 400　　　B. 20　　　C. 200　　　D. 500

20. Given the figure, which sides of triangle *CDE* are congruent?

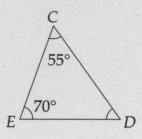

Note: Figure not drawn to scale.

  A. $\overline{CD}$ and $\overline{DE}$

  B. $\overline{DE}$ and $\overline{EC}$

  C. $\overline{EC}$ and $\overline{CD}$

  D. $\overline{EC}$, $\overline{CD}$, $\overline{DE}$

21. If the triangle below underwent the translation $T_{(4,-3)}$, what would the coordinates of *m'* be?

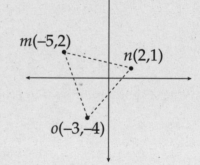

Note: Figure not drawn to scale.

  A. (4,–3)

  B. (2,–5)

  C. (–1,–1)

  D. (2,1)

22. If you compare the four numbered angles in the figure, which angle has the smallest tangent?

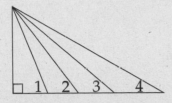

Note: Figure not drawn to scale.

A. 1　　　　B. 2　　　　C. 3　　　　D. 4

23. If a basketball is flattened into a circle and the circumference is 6π, what was the surface area of the basketball before it was flattened?

A. 36π　　　B. 72π　　　C. 12π　　　D. 180π

24. In the figure, the shadow of the flagpole makes an angle of 25° with the ground. The flagpole is perpendicular to the ground. What is the measure of $\angle a$?

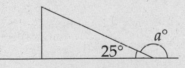

Note: Figure not drawn to scale.

A.　90°　　　B. 155°　　　C. 25°　　　D. 125°

25. Given the figure, which of the following is not a possible length of $\overline{AB}$?

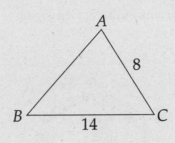

Note: Figure not drawn to scale.

A. 5　　　　B. 7　　　　C. 14　　　　D. 20

26. If the height of a rectangle is 4 and its area is 12, what is the length of its diagonal?

A.　5

B.　$\sqrt{80} \approx 8.9$

C.　$\sqrt{160} \approx 12.6$

D.　$\sqrt{208} \approx 14.4$

27. In the figure, BC is a diameter; the measure of minor arc $AB = 60°$; $AC = 4\sqrt{3}$

What is the area of the shaded region (in square units)?

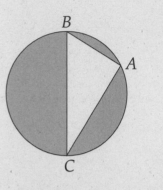

Note: Figure not drawn to scale.

A. 16π

B. $16\pi - 8\sqrt{3}$

C. $16\pi - 4\sqrt{3}$

D. $8\sqrt{3} - 16\pi$

28. What is the area of circle m (in square units)?

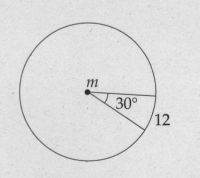

Note: Figure not drawn to scale.

A. 144   B. 144π C. $5,184\pi$ D. 1,650

29. A cube has volume 600 cm³. What is its surface area to the nearest tenth?

A. 423.4 cm²

B. 71.1 cm²

C. 600 cm²

D. 2,561.4 cm²

30. In the figure, $\triangle X'Y'Z'$ is the image of $\triangle XYZ$ after being rotated 180° about point X. What is the correct graph of $\triangle X'Y'Z'$?

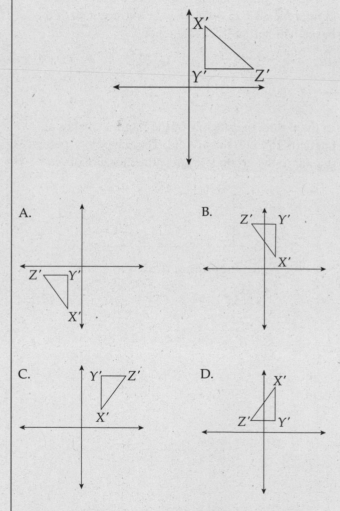

Note: Figure not drawn to scale.

SAMPLE GRIDDED-RESPONSE QUESTIONS FOR GEOMETRY

The following questions are similar to the multiple-choice questions, but answer choices are not provided. You must determine the answers yourself using separate scratch paper, and then use a special area on the answer sheet like the one shown here to bubble in your answers. If the answer is a mixed numeral, it is to be gridded as a decimal or improper fraction (e.g., 3 1/2 should be gridded as 7/2 or 3.5).

Grid your response to items #1 through #5 below. Use the decimal (.) or the fraction sign (/) if your answers require it.

Examples of how to grid your answers

TEST ONE, DAY TWO

1. In the figure, ray *a* is an angle bisector, and lines *b* and *c* are parallel. What is the value of $z - x$?

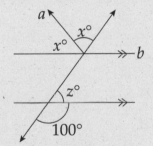

Note: Figure not drawn to scale.

2. In the figure, what is the value of the hypotenuse to the nearest tenth?

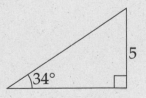

Note: Figure not drawn to scale.

3. If the base of a parallelogram is 100 and the height is 20, what is the area?

4. The figure, a regular pentagon is inscribed within a circle. What is the measure of $\angle C$, in degrees?

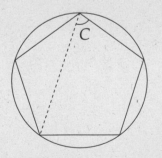

Note: Figure not drawn to scale.

5. What is the slope of a line which is defined by the points $(-3,8)$ and $(5,12)$?

Written Response Question

1. Circle L has a diameter of 8. MN is tangent to the circle, and the length of NP is 6. Explain how to find the measure of $\angle L$, $\angle M$, and $\angle N$. Specify each idea you use.

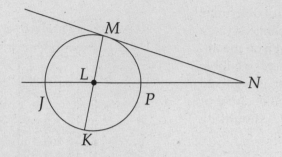

Note: Figure not drawn to scale.

Remember to show all parts of your solution, and explain how you arrived at your answer.

ANSWER KEY TO GEOMETRY PRACTICE TEST ONE

Day One Questions: **Day Two Questions:**

1	C	
2	B	
3	D	
4	A	
5	B	
6	B	
7	C	
8	C	
9	A	
10	D	
11	B	
12	C	
13	B	
14	C	
15	A	
16	A	
17	C	
18	C	
19	A	
20	B	
21	C	
22	D	
23	A	
24	B	
25	A	
26	A	
27	B	
28	C	
29	A	
30	B	

Grid-Ins:

1 30
2 8.9
3 2,000
4 72
5 .5 or 1/2

Written Response:

1 See explanations for a properly credited response.

GRID-IN ANSWER SHEET

1

⊘	⊘	⊘	⊘	⊘
.	.	.	.	.
⓪	⓪	⓪	⓪	⓪
①	①	①	①	①
②	②	②	②	②
③	③	③	③	③
④	④	④	④	④
⑤	⑤	⑤	⑤	⑤
⑥	⑥	⑥	⑥	⑥
⑦	⑦	⑦	⑦	⑦
⑧	⑧	⑧	⑧	⑧
⑨	⑨	⑨	⑨	⑨

2

⊘	⊘	⊘	⊘	⊘
.	.	.	.	.
⓪	⓪	⓪	⓪	⓪
①	①	①	①	①
②	②	②	②	②
③	③	③	③	③
④	④	④	④	④
⑤	⑤	⑤	⑤	⑤
⑥	⑥	⑥	⑥	⑥
⑦	⑦	⑦	⑦	⑦
⑧	⑧	⑧	⑧	⑧
⑨	⑨	⑨	⑨	⑨

3

⊘	⊘	⊘	⊘	⊘
.	.	.	.	.
⓪	⓪	⓪	⓪	⓪
①	①	①	①	①
②	②	②	②	②
③	③	③	③	③
④	④	④	④	④
⑤	⑤	⑤	⑤	⑤
⑥	⑥	⑥	⑥	⑥
⑦	⑦	⑦	⑦	⑦
⑧	⑧	⑧	⑧	⑧
⑨	⑨	⑨	⑨	⑨

4

⊘	⊘	⊘	⊘	⊘
.	.	.	.	.
⓪	⓪	⓪	⓪	⓪
①	①	①	①	①
②	②	②	②	②
③	③	③	③	③
④	④	④	④	④
⑤	⑤	⑤	⑤	⑤
⑥	⑥	⑥	⑥	⑥
⑦	⑦	⑦	⑦	⑦
⑧	⑧	⑧	⑧	⑧
⑨	⑨	⑨	⑨	⑨

5

⊘	⊘	⊘	⊘	⊘
.	.	.	.	.
⓪	⓪	⓪	⓪	⓪
①	①	①	①	①
②	②	②	②	②
③	③	③	③	③
④	④	④	④	④
⑤	⑤	⑤	⑤	⑤
⑥	⑥	⑥	⑥	⑥
⑦	⑦	⑦	⑦	⑦
⑧	⑧	⑧	⑧	⑧
⑨	⑨	⑨	⑨	⑨

6

⊘	⊘	⊘	⊘	⊘
.	.	.	.	.
⓪	⓪	⓪	⓪	⓪
①	①	①	①	①
②	②	②	②	②
③	③	③	③	③
④	④	④	④	④
⑤	⑤	⑤	⑤	⑤
⑥	⑥	⑥	⑥	⑥
⑦	⑦	⑦	⑦	⑦
⑧	⑧	⑧	⑧	⑧
⑨	⑨	⑨	⑨	⑨

7

⊘	⊘	⊘	⊘	⊘
.	.	.	.	.
⓪	⓪	⓪	⓪	⓪
①	①	①	①	①
②	②	②	②	②
③	③	③	③	③
④	④	④	④	④
⑤	⑤	⑤	⑤	⑤
⑥	⑥	⑥	⑥	⑥
⑦	⑦	⑦	⑦	⑦
⑧	⑧	⑧	⑧	⑧
⑨	⑨	⑨	⑨	⑨

8

⊘	⊘	⊘	⊘	⊘
.	.	.	.	.
⓪	⓪	⓪	⓪	⓪
①	①	①	①	①
②	②	②	②	②
③	③	③	③	③
④	④	④	④	④
⑤	⑤	⑤	⑤	⑤
⑥	⑥	⑥	⑥	⑥
⑦	⑦	⑦	⑦	⑦
⑧	⑧	⑧	⑧	⑧
⑨	⑨	⑨	⑨	⑨

9

⊘	⊘	⊘	⊘	⊘
.	.	.	.	.
⓪	⓪	⓪	⓪	⓪
①	①	①	①	①
②	②	②	②	②
③	③	③	③	③
④	④	④	④	④
⑤	⑤	⑤	⑤	⑤
⑥	⑥	⑥	⑥	⑥
⑦	⑦	⑦	⑦	⑦
⑧	⑧	⑧	⑧	⑧
⑨	⑨	⑨	⑨	⑨

10

⊘	⊘	⊘	⊘	⊘
.	.	.	.	.
⓪	⓪	⓪	⓪	⓪
①	①	①	①	①
②	②	②	②	②
③	③	③	③	③
④	④	④	④	④
⑤	⑤	⑤	⑤	⑤
⑥	⑥	⑥	⑥	⑥
⑦	⑦	⑦	⑦	⑦
⑧	⑧	⑧	⑧	⑧
⑨	⑨	⑨	⑨	⑨

Completely darken bubbles with a No. 2 pencil. If you make a mistake, be sure to erase mark completely. Erase all stray marks.

Practice Test One

1. Ⓐ Ⓑ Ⓒ Ⓓ
2. Ⓕ Ⓖ Ⓗ Ⓙ
3. Ⓐ Ⓑ Ⓒ Ⓓ
4. Ⓕ Ⓖ Ⓗ Ⓙ
5. Ⓐ Ⓑ Ⓒ Ⓓ
6. Ⓕ Ⓖ Ⓗ Ⓙ
7. Ⓐ Ⓑ Ⓒ Ⓓ
8. Ⓕ Ⓖ Ⓗ Ⓙ
9. Ⓐ Ⓑ Ⓒ Ⓓ
10. Ⓕ Ⓖ Ⓗ Ⓙ
11. Ⓐ Ⓑ Ⓒ Ⓓ
12. Ⓕ Ⓖ Ⓗ Ⓙ
13. Ⓐ Ⓑ Ⓒ Ⓓ
14. Ⓕ Ⓖ Ⓗ Ⓙ

15. Ⓐ Ⓑ Ⓒ Ⓓ
16. Ⓕ Ⓖ Ⓗ Ⓙ
17. Ⓐ Ⓑ Ⓒ Ⓓ
18. Ⓕ Ⓖ Ⓗ Ⓙ
19. Ⓐ Ⓑ Ⓒ Ⓓ
20. Ⓕ Ⓖ Ⓗ Ⓙ
21. Ⓐ Ⓑ Ⓒ Ⓓ
22. Ⓕ Ⓖ Ⓗ Ⓙ
23. Ⓐ Ⓑ Ⓒ Ⓓ
24. Ⓕ Ⓖ Ⓗ Ⓙ
25. Ⓐ Ⓑ Ⓒ Ⓓ
26. Ⓕ Ⓖ Ⓗ Ⓙ
27. Ⓐ Ⓑ Ⓒ Ⓓ

PRACTICE TEST ONE EXPLANATIONS

1. In the figure, $\angle l$ and $\angle m$ are supplementary, $\angle m$ and $\angle n$ are supplementary, $\angle n$ and $\angle o$ are complementary, and the measure of $\angle o$ is 36°. What is the measure of $\angle l$?

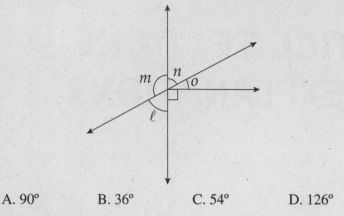

A. 90°   B. 36°   C. 54°   D. 126°

C. is the correct answer. Since $\angle n$ and $\angle o$ are <u>complementary</u>, then $90 - m\angle o = m\angle n$. By substituting for $m\angle o$ (36°), you can solve for $m\angle n$ (54°). Next notice that $\angle n$ and $\angle l$ are <u>vertical angles</u>, and thus congruent. Therefore, $m\angle l = 54°$.

2. In the figure, if line a and line b are parallel, what is the measurement of $\angle x$?

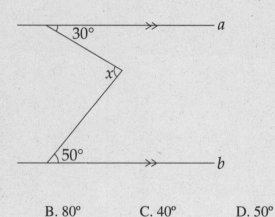

A. 60°   B. 80°   C. 40°   D. 50°

B. is the correct answer. There are a number of ways to solve this problem, but we will demonstrate one way that utilizes your knowledge of triangles. Construct a perpendicular line that creates three triangles, like this:

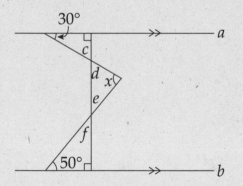

Since the angles of a triangle sum to 180°, we know that $m\angle c = 60°$ and $m\angle f = 40°$. $\angle d$ is a vertical angle of $\angle c$, so its measure also equals 60°, and $\angle e$ is a vertical angle of $\angle f$, so its measure equals 40°. Lastly, to solve for the value of $\angle x$, once again use the knowledge that the sum of the angles in a triangle equals 180°. $m\angle x = 180° - 60° - 40°$, or 80°.

3. There are three shapes in the figure: regular pentagon *ABCDH*, right triangle *HDG*, and square *DGEF*. What is the degree measure of ∠*CDE*?

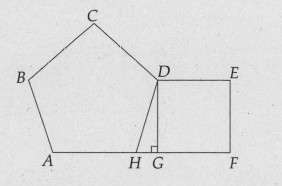

A. 126° B. 234° C. 198° D. 144°

D. is the correct answer. To solve this problem, you need to remember that the degree measure of an angle in a regular polygon = $180° (n - 2)/n$, where n = number of sides.

Since *ABCDH* is a pentagon, you know there are 5 sides, and so each angle inside the pentagon = $180° (5 - 2)/5 = 108°$. Therefore, you know that m∠*AHD* = 108°. You can then figure out that m∠*DHG* is 180° − 108° = 72°, because they are supplementary angles.

Since m∠*DHG* is a right triangle, you can then determine the degree measure of ∠*HDG*. Since the angles of a triangle add up to 180°, simply subtract 90° and 72° from 180° and you get 18°.

Now, you can calculate the degree measure of ∠*CDE*.

You know that the total degrees around point *D* is 360°.

Therefore, m∠*CDH* + m∠*HDG* + m∠*GDE* + m∠*CDE* = 360°. Now plug in the numbers:

108° + 18° + 90° + m−*CDE* = 360°

m∠*CDE* = 144°

4. In the triangle, what is the value of x?

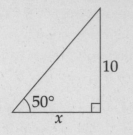

A. 10/(tan 50)

B. (tan 50)/10

C. 10 • tan 50

D. 1/(10 • tan 50)

A. is the correct answer. tan x = opposite/adjacent, so:

tan 50 = 10/x

(tan 50)x = 10

x = 10/(tan 50)

5. In the figure, $\overline{AD}$ and $\overline{GE}$ are diameters of the circle O. What is the degree measure of arc CD?

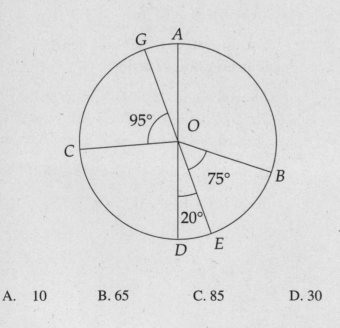

A. 10   B. 65   C. 85   D. 30

B. is the correct answer. m∠AOG is a vertical angle to ∠DOE, so it also measures 20°.
∠AOC is the sum of ∠AOG and ∠GOC, so it equals 115°. ∠AOC and ∠COD are supplementary, so m∠COD = 65°, and the arc it subtends, m$\overarc{CD}$, is also 65°.

6. In the figure, if the perimeter of the parallelogram is 120, and *EB* = 10, what is *AB*?

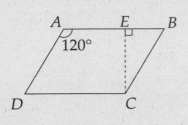

A. 80   B.   40   C.   30   D. 12

B. is the correct answer. Perimeter of a parallelogram = $2l + 2w$, so the perimeter of this parallelogram would be $2(AB) + 2(BC)$.

First, we must find m∠*EBC*. Since any two angles subsequent angles of a parallelogram add up to 180°, we know that ∠*EBC* equals 60°. Since ∠*BEC* is a 90° angle, then triangle *EBC* is a 30-60-90 special triangle. Therefore, if *EB* equals 10, then *BC* equals 20.

We can now determine *AB* by plugging *BC* into the perimeter equation.

Perimeter = $2(AB) + 2(BC) = 2(AB)$
$2(20)\,120$
$AB = 40$

7. What is the surface area of the cube in the figure?

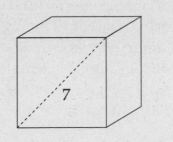

A. 294   B. 588   C. 147   D. 49

C. is the correct answer. The surface area of a cube = $6s^2$. You are given the diagonal of one side of the cube. You should know by now that if 7 is the diagonal of a square, then each side of the square equals $7\sqrt{2}$. You then plug this into the area equation. Area = $6s^2 = 6(7\sqrt{2})^2 = 6(49/2) = 147$.

8. What is the area of the triangle with vertices (–7,0), (–4,0), and (–5,5)?

   A. 25 square units

   B. 20 square units

   C. 7.5 square units

   D. 5.5 square unitsC.

C. is the correct answer. Here is a picture of the triangle described in the question:

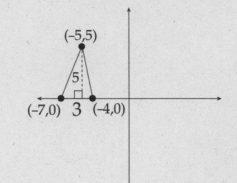

The formula for the area of a triangle is 1/2 *bh*. The base of this triangle is 3 units long and the height is 5 units long, so the area is 1/2 (3 × 5), or 7.5 square units.

9. What is the measure of ∠*BAM*?

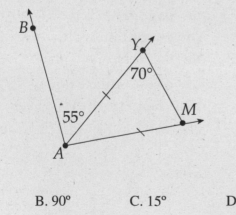

A. 95°   B. 90°   C. 15°   D. 98°

A. is the correct answer. $\overline{YA}$ and $\overline{MA}$ are congruent, so $\triangle YAM$ is an isosceles triangle. Thus ∠*Y* and ∠*M* are congruent. m∠*YAM* = 180° – 70° = 40°. m∠*BAM* is equal to the sum of m∠*BAY* and m∠*YAM*, so m∠*BAM* = 55° + 40° = 95°.

10. What is the measure of ∠ABC to the nearest tenth?

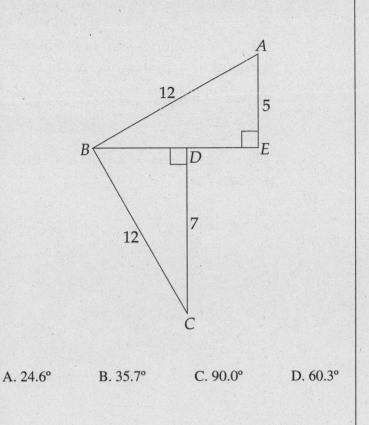

A. 24.6°   B. 35.7°   C. 90.0°   D. 60.3°

D. is the correct answer. Use trigo-
    nometry to solve for the measures
    of ∠ABE and ∠DBC. Then, com-
    bine these values to get the measure
    of ∠ABC.

    sin ∠ABE = 5/12

    ∠ABE = sin⁻¹(5/12)

    m∠ABE ≈ 24.6

    sin ∠DBC = 7/12

    ∠DBC = sin⁻¹(7/12)

    m∠DBC ≈ 35.7

    m∠ABE + m∠DBC = m∠ABC

    24.6 + 35.7 = 60.3

    m∠ABC ≈ 60.3

11. In the figure, if $\overline{AC}$ and $\overline{BD}$ are diameters, $AC = 20$,
    and the measure of ∠AOD = 100°, what is the length
    of the arc AB?

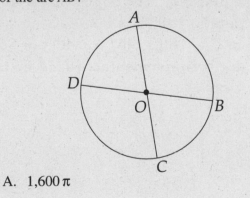

A. 1,600 π

B. $4\frac{4}{9}\pi$

C. 90 π

D. 10 π

B. is the correct answer. The length of
    an arc = (angle/360) ∠∂. Since you
    know that m∠AOD = 100°, then
    m∠AOB = 80° (they are supple-
    mentary). Use 80° in the arc length
    equation: length = (80/360) ×
    $\pi(20) = 4\frac{4}{9}\pi.$

12. What is the surface area of a right circular cone with a diameter of 10 and a height of 15 (in square units)?

   A. 150

   B. 150π

   C. 104π

   D. $1,500\pi$

C. is the correct answer. The surface area of a right circular cone equals $\pi r(r + \delta)$. δ equals the slant of the cone. You can determine the slant by using the Pythagorean Theorem:

radius² + height² = slant²

$5^2 + 15^2 = \delta^2$ $\delta \approx 15.8$

The surface area $= \pi (5) (5 + 15.8)$
$\approx 104\pi$

13. In the figure, $a - b =$

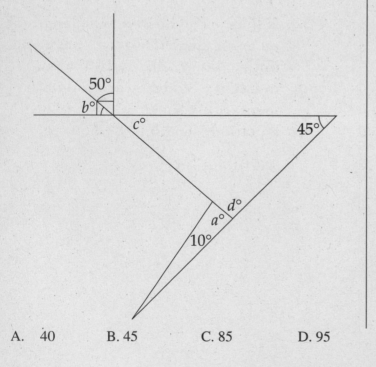

A. 40   B. 45   C. 85   D. 95

B. is the correct answer. $\angle b$ is complementary with the 50° angle, so its measure equals 40°. $\angle c$ is a vertical angle to $\angle b$, so its measure also equals 40°. The angles in a triangle sum to 180°, so $m\angle \partial = 180° - 45° - \angle 40°$, or 95°. $\angle a$ is supplementary to $\angle \partial$, so $m\angle a = 85°$.

$a - b = 85 - 40$, or 45.

14. A square is circumscribed within a circle with a radius of 4. What is the area of the shaded region (in square units)?

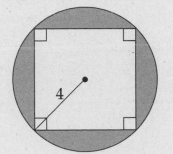

4

A. $16\pi^2$

B. 16π

C. $16\pi - 32$

D. $16\pi + 32$

C. is the correct answer. The shaded region is the area of the circle minus the area of the square:

Area of the circle = $\pi(4)^2$

Area of the circle = 16π

Area of the square = $\frac{1}{2}$ (product of the diagonals, which measure 8 each)

Area of the square = $\frac{1}{2}(64)$

Area of the square = 32

Area of the shaded region = $16\pi - 32$ square units

15. In the figure, ABC is an equilateral triangle. In addition, $\overline{BC}$ and $\overline{DE}$ are parallel. If $AE = 40$, what is DE?

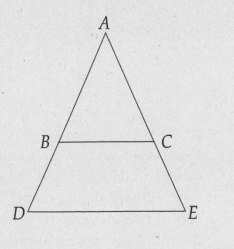

A. 40   B. $40/\sqrt{3}$ C. 20   D. 60

A. is the correct answer. Since $\triangle ABC$ is equilateral, and $\overline{BC}$ and $\overline{DE}$ are parallel, $\triangle ADE$ is also an equilateral triangle. The sides of an equilateral triangle are congruent and the measure of each angle equals 60°, so each side of $\triangle ADE$ measures 40.

16. If the measure of the largest angle of an isosceles triangle is 122° and its longest side is 40, what is the length of its other two sides to the nearest tenth?

A. 22.9   B. 17.5   C. 15.5   D. 34.2

A.   is the correct answer. Since the longest side of a triangle is always opposite the largest angle, you can draw the following figure to help solve for the missing sides:

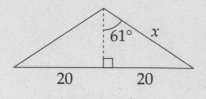

$\sin 61 = 20/x$

$(x)\sin 61 = 20$

$x \approx 20/(\sin 61)$

$x \approx 22.9$

17. What are the coordinates of the point (3,5) reflected by the y-axis?

    A. (−3,−5)

    B. (3,−5)

    C. (−3,5)

    D. (5,3)

C.   is the correct answer.

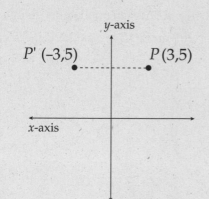

In this case, the y-axis is acting as a mirror, in which case the sign of the x-coordinate changes, and the y-coordinate remains the same. Thus, the reflected point is located at (−3,5).

18. If the volume of a right hexagonal prism is 3,444 cubic units, its height is 12 units, and the perimeter of the hexagonal base is 82 units, what is the length of its apothem?

A. 4 B. 24 C. 7 D. 32

C. is the correct answer. The volume of any right prism = $(1/2\ ap)h$. a, you should remember, stands for apothem, and p is perimeter of the base. You are given the volume, p, and h. All you need to do is plug in the numbers and solve for the apothem.

$$3{,}444 = (1/2)\ a\ (82)(12)$$

$$a = 7$$

19. In the figure, ABF and ACE are similar triangles. The length of $\overline{AB}$ is one-fourth the length of $\overline{AC}$. What is the area of the square (in square units)?

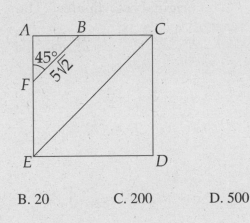

A. 400 B. 20 C. 200 D. 500

A. is the correct answer. Since ABF is a 45-45-90 triangle, you know that $AB = 5$, according to the special properties of that kind of triangle. Since AB is

$$\frac{1}{4}\ (AC),\ AC = 4(AB) = 4(5) = 20.$$

Two triangles that share a hypotenuse as demonstrated in the figure make a square. That means that all sides equal 20. The area of a square $= s^2$. Therefore, the area $= (20)^2 = 400$ square units.

20. Given the figure, which sides of triangle *CDE* are congruent?

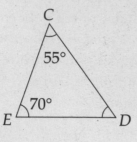

A. $\overline{CD}$ and $\overline{DE}$

B. $\overline{DE}$ and $\overline{EC}$

C. $\overline{EC}$ and $\overline{CD}$

D. $\overline{EC}$, $\overline{CD}$, $\overline{DE}$

B. is the correct answer. First, solve for the missing angle by subtracting the known angles from 180. $180 - 70 - 55 = 55$. Both $\overline{DE}$ and $\overline{EC}$ are opposite the 55° angles. Therefore, the sides are congruent as well.

21. If the triangle below underwent the translation $T_{(4,-3)}$, what would the coordinates of *m′* be?

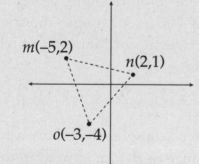

A. (4,–3)

B. (2,–5)

C. (–1,–1)

D. (2,1)

C. is the correct answer. Remember that a translation simply moves a set of points to a new location. The new location can be determined by adding the translated coordinates to the original coordinates. Thus, *m′* equals:

$(-5 + 4, 2 - 3)$ or $(-1,-1)$

22. If you compare the four numbered angles in the figure, which angle has the smallest tangent?

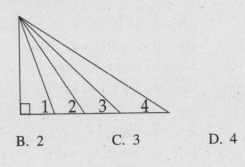

A. 1   B. 2   C. 3   D. 4

D. is the correct answer. tan x = opposite/adjacent. In this example, the opposite sides are all the same, so the angle with the largest adjacent side will have the smallest tangent, because it will make the denominator the largest in the tangent ratio.

23. If a basketball is flattened into a circle and the circumference is 6π, what was the surface area of the basketball before it was flattened?

A. 36π B. 72π C. 12π D. 180π

A. is the correct answer. The surface area of a sphere = $4\pi r^2$. Therefore, you need to find the radius. You are not given the radius, but you are given the circumference. You can find the radius by using the equation for circumference of a circle.

Circumference = $2\pi r$; $6\pi = 2\pi r$; $r = 3$

Now that you have the radius, plug it into the SA equation.

$SA = 4\pi(3)^2 = 36\pi$ square units

24. In the figure, the shadow of the flagpole makes an angle of 25° with the ground. The flagpole is perpendicular to the ground. What is the measure of $\angle a$?

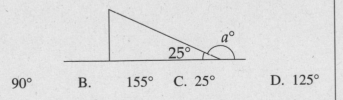

A. 90°   B. 155°   C. 25°   D. 125°

B. is the correct answer. $\angle a$ is supplementary to the 25° angle, which means that their sum is 180°. Therefore, m$\angle a$ = 155°.

25. Given the figure, which of the following is not a possible length of $\overline{AB}$?

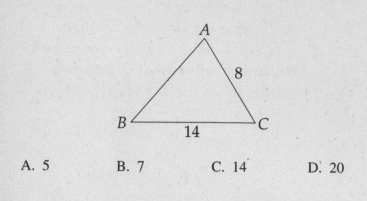

A. 5   B. 7   C. 14   D. 20

A. is the correct answer. 5 is too small a length. The parameters for how long a side of a triangle could be, given the other two lengths, is that the side cannot be longer than the sum of the two other sides, and it cannot be shorter than the difference between the two other sides. $14 + 8 = 22$, $14 - 8 = 6$. Any number between 6 and 22 is fine, but 5 is not.

26. If the height of a rectangle is 4 and its area is 12, what is the length of its diagonal?

A. 5

B. $\sqrt{80} \approx 8.9$

C. $\sqrt{160} \approx 12.6$

D. $\sqrt{280} \approx 14.4$

A. is the correct answer. Area of a rectangle = height × width. Plug in the numbers. $12 = 4 \times$ width; width $= 3$. If you draw the diagonal, you have made two triangles with sides 3 and 4. Using the Pythagorean Theorem, $3^2 + 4^2 = x^2$; $x = 5$.

27. In the figure, BC is a diameter; the measure of minor arc $AB = 60°$; $AC = 4\sqrt{3}$. What is the area of the shaded region (in square units)?

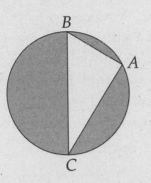

A. 16π

B. $16\pi - 8\sqrt{3}$

C. $16\pi - 4\sqrt{3}$

D. $8\sqrt{3} - 16\pi$

B. is the correct answer. The shaded region is the area of the circle minus the area of the triangle. $\triangle ACB$ subtends arc AB, so its measure is $\frac{1}{2}$ of arc AB, or $30°$. $\angle CAB$ subtends arc CB, which measures $180°$ (because it is a diameter), so the measure of $\angle CAB$ is $90°$ (half of $180°$).

DABC is a 30-60-90 right triangle.

The area of a circle is πr^2. In this case, it is $4^2\pi$, or 16π square units.

The area of the triangle: $\frac{1}{2}(4\sqrt{3} \times 4) = 8\sqrt{3}$ square units

The area of the shaded region: $16\pi - 8\sqrt{3}$ square units

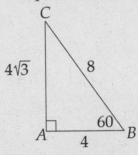

In a $30 - 60 - 90$ right triangle, the shorter leg equals the lower leg divided by $\sqrt{3}$, and the hypotenuse is twice the shorter leg. Use the length of $\overline{BC}$ (which is a diameter) to solve for the area of the circle.

28. What is the area of circle *m* (in square units)?

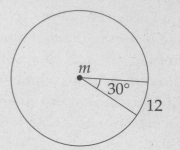

    A. 144

    B. 144 π

    C. 5,184 π

    D. 1,650

C. is the correct answer. In order to find the area, you need the radius. However, in order to get the radius, you must calculate the circumference. You know, from the figure, that a 30° sector has a circumference of 12. 360° is 12 times 30°. Therefore, the total circumference is 12 times 12 = 144. Then, you find the radius using circumference = $2\pi r$

$$144 = 2\pi r \qquad\qquad r = 72/\pi$$

Now, you are able to calculate the area of the circle = $\pi r^2 = \pi(72/\pi)^2 = 5,184\ \pi$ square units

29. A cube has volume 600 cm³. What is its surface area to the nearest tenth?

    A. 426.8 cm²

    B. 71.1 cm²

    C. 600 cm²

    D. 2,561.4 cm²

A. is the correct answer. The volume of a cube = s^3. Therefore, since the volume equals 600, each side equals approximately 8.4. Plug that number into the surface area equation: $SA = 6s^2 = 6(8.4)^2 = 426.8$ cm²

30. In the figure, $\triangle X'Y'Z'$ is the image of $\triangle XYZ$ after being rotated 180° about point X. What is the correct graph of $\triangle X'Y'Z'$?

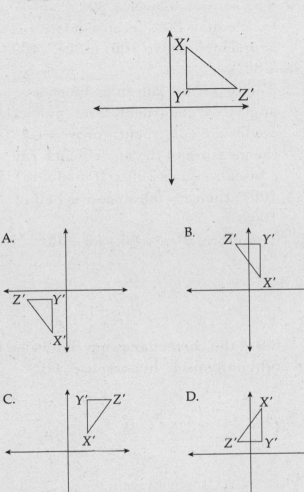

A.

B.

C.

D.

B. is the correct answer. First off, since the rotation occurs about point X (and NOT the origin), then X' will be in the same location as X. From this we can eliminate choice A right off the bat.

In order to select the correct answer, it may be useful to realize that a 180° rotation is the same as a point reflection. In other words, the lines connected to point X can be extended through X to create their rotated images:

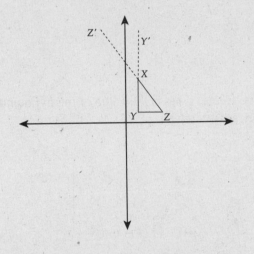

After drawing in the locations of Y' and Z', it becomes obvious that B is the correct answer.

TEST ONE, DAY TWO

1. In the figure, ray *a* is an angle bisector, and lines *b* and *c* are parallel. What is the value of $z - x$?

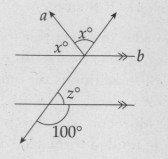

The correct answer is 30.
m$\angle z$ equals 80°, because it is supplementary to 100° (180° − 100° = 80°).
The two rules "alternate interior angles are congruent," and "vertical angles are congruent," prove that the measure of the angle which ray *a* bisects equals 100°. If it equals 100Υ, then *x* = 50, since *x* is half of 100°.
Therefore, $z - x = 80 - 50 = 30$.

2. In the figure, what is the value of the hypotenuse to the nearest tenth?

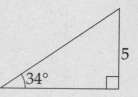

8.9 is the correct answer. Sin 34° = 5/hypotenuse; hypotenuse ≈ 8.9

3. If the base of a parallelogram is 100 and the height is 20, what is the area (in square units)?

2,000 is the correct answer. The equation for area of a parallelogram is base × height. Plug in 100 × 20 = 2,000 square units.

4. The figure, a regular pentagon is inscribed within a circle. What is the measure of ∠C, in degrees?

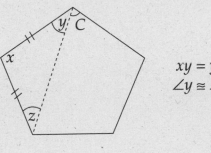

$$xy = yz$$
$$\angle y \cong \angle z$$

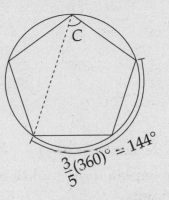

$$\tfrac{3}{5}(360)° = 144°$$

72 is the correct answer. The circle in the figure can be used in the solution, but it is not necessary. Since each of the angles in a regular polygon has a measure of $180(n - 2)/n$ (where n equals the number of sides), each angle in the regular pentagon in the diagram equals $180(5 - 2)/5 = 108°$. Since the sides of a regular pentagon are all equal, the dotted line in the figure creates the following isoceles triangle:

$\angle x = 108°$, so the remaining two congruent angles each equal $36°$ ($36 + 36 + 108 = 180$).

$$\angle C = 108 - 36 = 72°$$

If you forget the formula for determining the measure of the angles in a regular polygon, you can use your knowledge of inscribed angles to determine the measure of ∠C. Inscribed angles are half the measure of the arcs they subtend.

$$\tfrac{1}{2}(144)° = 72°.$$

5. What is the slope of a line which is defined by the points $(-3,8)$ and $(5,12)$?

.5 or $\tfrac{1}{2}$ is the correct answer. Use the slope formula to determine the slope.

$(8 - 12)/(-3 - 5) = -4/-8 = \tfrac{1}{2}$

Written Response Question

1. Circle L has a diameter of 8. MN is tangent to the circle, and the length of NP is 6. Explain how to find the measure of $\angle L$, $\angle M$, and $\angle N$. Specify each idea you use.

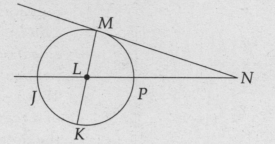

Remember to show all parts of your solution, and explain how you arrived at your answer.

SAMPLE RESPONSE RECEIVING A SCORE OF 3 OR 4

$\angle M = 90°$ (definition of the angle formed at the intersection of a tangent and diameter)

$LM = 4$ (half of diameter)

$LP = 4$ (half of diameter)

$PN = 6$ (given)

$LN = 10$ ($LP + PN$)

$\cos L = 4/10$

$\angle L = 66.4°$

$\angle N = 180° - 90° - 66.4° = 23.6°$ (The angles of a triangle sum to 180°.)

This response is accurate and complete. However, the explanation could be slightly more detailed, so it may not receive the possible four points.

SAMPLE RESPONSE RECEIVING A SCORE OF 2

$\angle M = 90°$ (right angle)

$LM = 4$

$LN = 10$

$\sin L = 4/10$

$L = 23.6$

$N = 90 - 23.6 = 66.4$

This response demonstrates knowledge in the area, but the explanation is severely limited. Additionally, the error of using of the sine function instead of cosine limits the score this response will receive.

(Note: This is a classic case of where the student could have received additional points by explaining each step. Remember: Show all of your work on the appropriate answer sheet.)

PRACTICE TEST TWO

SAMPLE MULTIPLE-CHOICE QUESTIONS FOR GEOMETRY

Make sure you have two or three No. 2 pencils with erasers and a ruler or straightedge available to you during the exam. You also may have a calculator; it may be either a scientific or graphing calculator. You may not use minicomputers, pocket organizers, or calculators with QWERTY (typewriter) keyboards. You may not share your calculator with other students.

Do not spend too much time on a question that seems too difficult. Answer the easier questions first and then return to the harder ones if you have the time. Try to answer every question, even if you have to guess.

Notes: (1) Figures that accompany problems are drawn as accurately as possible EXCEPT when it is stated that a figure is not drawn to scale. All figures lie in a plane unless otherwise indicated.

(2) All numbers used are real numbers. All algebraic expressions represent real numbers unless otherwise indicated.

TEST TWO, DAY ONE

1. What is the volume of a cone with diameter 23 and height 40 (in cubic units)?

    A. $2,645\pi$

    B. 460π

    C. 920π

    D. $5,290\pi$

2. In the figure, what is the value of X?

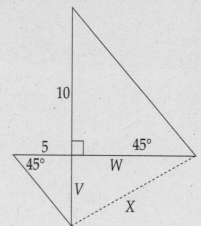

Note: Figure not drawn to scale.

    A. $\sqrt{200}$

    B. $\sqrt{15}$

    C. $\sqrt{50}$

    D. $\sqrt{125}$

3. Laura Anne cuts half of a pie into three equal pieces, and the other half into four equal pieces. If the area of one of the smaller pieces is π/2, what is the area of one of the larger pieces?

A. 2π/3

B. 3π/8

C. π

D. 1/8(π)

4. What is the perimeter of a regular decagon if one side is 24?

A. 172   B. 240   C. 24   D. 2,400

5. If a cube with side 8 had the same volume as a sphere, what would the sphere's radius be, to the nearest tenth?

A. 8.2   B. 5.0   C. 4.3   D. 2.4

6. In the figure, what is the measurement of ∠A?

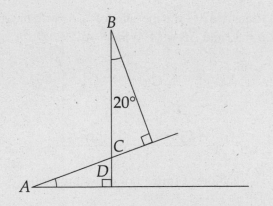

Note: Figure not drawn to scale.

A. 70°   B. 50°   C. 20°   D. 30°

7. If ray *a* bisects ∠*b*, and the measurement of ∠*c* is 110°, what is the measurement of ∠*d*?

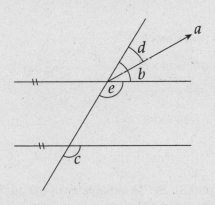

Note: Figure not drawn to scale.

A. 65°   B. 35°   C. 20°   D. 75°

8. In the figure, which side has length $16\sqrt{2}$?

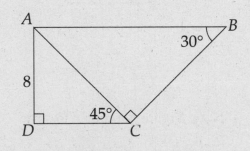

Note: Figure not drawn to scale.

A. $\overline{AB}$ B. $\overline{BC}$ C. $\overline{CD}$ D. $\overline{AD}$

9. In triangle *ABC*, the measure of an exterior angle drawn at *C* is four times the measure of ∠*B*. If the measure of ∠*A* = 33, what is the measure of ∠*B*?

A. 40°   B. 132°   C. 147°   D. 11°

10. In a store you see 2 cans of soup. Can A is 2 times as tall as Can B, and the radius of Can A is 1.3 times as large as Can B. How much more soup can be stored in Can A?

A. 2.6 times more

B. 3.4 times more

C. 1.7 times more

D. 3.3 times more

11. In the figure, if $\overline{EH}$ is a diameter of the circle, and it equals 42, and the length of the arc EFG is 33, then what is the measure of $\angle EFG$?

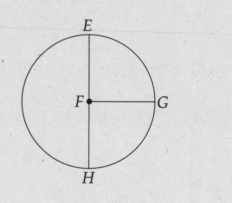

Note: Figure not drawn to scale.

A. 90°   B. 42°   C. 84°   D. 73°

12. What is the measure of arc x?

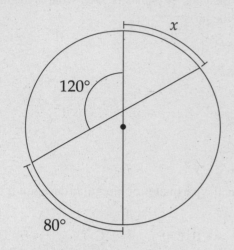

Note: Figure not drawn to scale.

A. 40°   B. 60°   C. 80°   D. 120°

13. $\angle ABC$ measures 78°, and is bisected by AD. What is the measure of angle ABD?

A. 78°   B. 12°   C. 102°   D. 39°

14. In triangle ABC, the measure of $\angle A = 45$, measure of $\angle B = 30$ and $CB = 24$. What is AC?

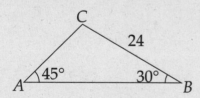

Note: Figure not drawn to scale.

A. $12\sqrt{3}$

B. $24\sqrt{2}$

C. $12\sqrt{2}$

D. $12\sqrt{5}$

15. What is the equation of the line defined by the points (–7,–4) and (1,1)?

    A. $y = 5/8x + 5/8$

    B. $y = 5/8x + 3/8$

    C. $y = 3/8x + 5/8$

    D. $y = 3/8x + 3/8$

16. In the figure, triangle *ABC* and triangle *DEF* are similar triangles. What is the length of *x*?

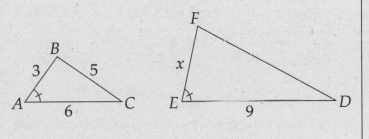

    Note: Figure not drawn to scale.

    A. 4.5   B. 5   C. 10   D. 15

17. In the figure, what is the area of the trapezoid (in square units)?

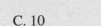
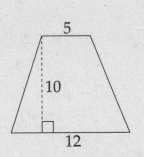

    Note: Figure not drawn to scale.

    A. 60   B. 30   C. 85   D. 150

18. In the figure, *r* and *s* are parallel lines, cut by transversals *t*, *u*, and *v* (*v* is perpendicular to *r* and *s*). If ∠2 and ∠3 are congruent, which angle is congruent to ∠16?

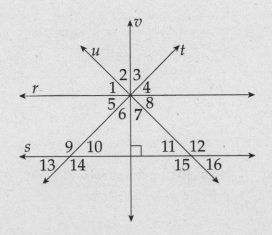

    Note: Figure not drawn to scale.

    A. ∠2   B. ∠4   C. ∠6   D. ∠9

19. In the figure, what is the measure of ∠*CAD*?

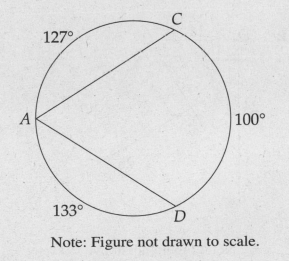

    Note: Figure not drawn to scale.

    A. 100   B. 63.5   C. 66.5   D. 50

20 What is the perimeter of the parallelogram in the figure?

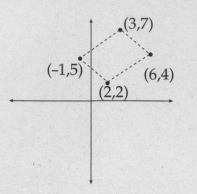

Note: Figure not drawn to scale.

A. 17.43

B. 16

C. 18.29

D. 75.89

21. What is the measure of ∠DAK?

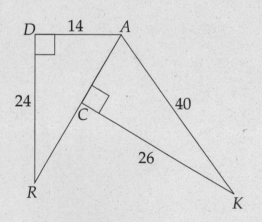

Note: Figure not drawn to scale.

A. 102.2

B. 40.5

C. 100.2

D. 59.7

22. In triangles *ABC* and *DEF*, *BC* = *EF*, *AB* = *DE*, and ∠*B* = ∠*E*. Which of the following is used to show that *ABC* and *DEF* are congruent?

A. SSS   B. ASA   C. SSA   D. SAS

23. What is the area of a 50 degree sector if the radius of the circle is 4 (in square units)?

A. 32π B. 2.2π C. 0.32π D. 8π

24. If a rectangular box does not have a lid, what is its surface area if its length is 12, width is 5, and height is 14 (in square units)?

A. 840   B. 718   C. 421   D. 596

25. What are the coordinates of the point (4,3) after being reflected about the origin?

A. (–3,–4)

B. (–4,3)

C. (3,–4)

D. (–4,–3)

26. How many triangles are shown in this figure?

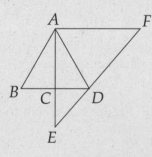

Note: Figure not drawn to scale.

A. 4   B. 5   C. 6   D. 7

27. If a regular polygon has 10 sides, what is the degree measure of each angle?

A. 180   B. 90   C. 144   D. 162

28. In the figure, what is the perimeter of the rhombus?

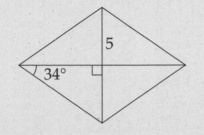

Note: Figure not drawn to scale.

A. 17   B. 11   C. 48   D. 36

29. How much liquid can be contained in a cylindrical pan if the surface area of the pan is $48\,\pi$ and the diameter is 8 (in cubed units)?

A. $32\,\pi$ B. $16\,\pi$ C. $64\,\pi$ D. $24\,\pi$

30. In the figure, $\triangle LMN$ has been dilated by a factor of 3. If the coordinates of M are (4,1), what are the coordinates of M'?

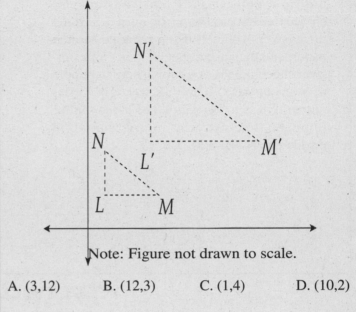

Note: Figure not drawn to scale.

A. (3,12)   B. (12,3)   C. (1,4)   D. (10,2)

SAMPLE GRIDDED-RESPONSE QUESTIONS
FOR GEOMETRY

The following questions are similar to the multiple-choice questions, but answer choices are not provided. You must determine the answers yourself using separate scratch paper, and then use a special area on the answer sheet like the one shown here to bubble in your answers. If the answer is a mixed numeral, it is to be gridded as a decimal or improper fraction (e.g., 3 1/2 should be gridded as 7/2 or 3.5).

Grid your response to items #1 through #5 below. Use the decimal (.) or the fraction sign (/) if your answers require it.

Examples of how to grid your answers

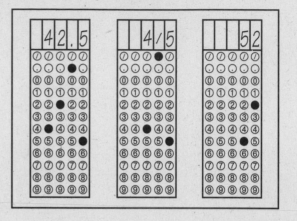

TEST TWO, DAY TWO

1. In the figure, ray *BC* bisects ∠*ABD*. What is the measure of ∠*ABD*?

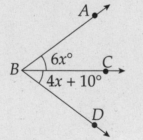

Note: Figure not drawn to scale.

2. In the figure, what is the value of *x* to the nearest tenth?

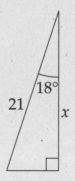

Note: Figure not drawn to scale.

3. In the figure, what is the area of the rhombus, in square units?

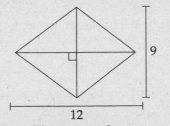

9

12

Note: Figure not drawn to scale.

4. If a regular polygon has 12 sides, what is the degree measure of each of its angles?

5. What is the volume of the shaded area to the nearest tenth, if the inner cylinder's radius is 4 and the outer cylinder's radius is 6 (in cubic units)?

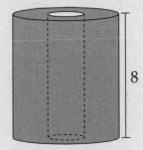

8

Note: Figure not drawn to scale.

Written Response Question

1. The vertices of the base of a regular pentagon are located at (1,1) and (4,1) on a Cartesian plane. Explain how to find the coordinates of the other three vertices. Specify each idea you use.

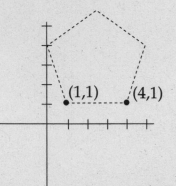

Note: Figure not drawn to scale.

Remember to show all parts of your solution, and explain how you arrived at your answer.

ANSWER KEY TO GEOMETRY PRACTICE TEST TWO

Day One Questions:

1 A
2 D
3 A
4 B
5 B
6 C
7 B
8 A
9 D
10 B
11 A
12 A
13 D
14 C
15 B
16 D
17 C
18 B
19 D
20 A
21 C
22 D
23 B
24 D
25 D
26 D
27 C
28 D
29 A
30 B

Day Two Questions:

Grid-Ins:

1 60
2 20.0
3 54
4 150
5 502.7

Written Response:

1 See explanations for a properly credited response.

GRID-IN ANSWER SHEET

1

2

3

4

5

6

7

8

9

10

Practice Test Two

1. Ⓐ Ⓑ Ⓒ Ⓓ
2. Ⓕ Ⓖ Ⓗ Ⓙ
3. Ⓐ Ⓑ Ⓒ Ⓓ
4. Ⓕ Ⓖ Ⓗ Ⓙ
5. Ⓐ Ⓑ Ⓒ Ⓓ
6. Ⓕ Ⓖ Ⓗ Ⓙ
7. Ⓐ Ⓑ Ⓒ Ⓓ
8. Ⓕ Ⓖ Ⓗ Ⓙ
9. Ⓐ Ⓑ Ⓒ Ⓓ
10. Ⓕ Ⓖ Ⓗ Ⓙ
11. Ⓐ Ⓑ Ⓒ Ⓓ
12. Ⓕ Ⓖ Ⓗ Ⓙ
13. Ⓐ Ⓑ Ⓒ Ⓓ
14. Ⓕ Ⓖ Ⓗ Ⓙ
15. Ⓐ Ⓑ Ⓒ Ⓓ
16. Ⓕ Ⓖ Ⓗ Ⓙ
17. Ⓐ Ⓑ Ⓒ Ⓓ
18. Ⓕ Ⓖ Ⓗ Ⓙ
19. Ⓐ Ⓑ Ⓒ Ⓓ
20. Ⓕ Ⓖ Ⓗ Ⓙ
21. Ⓐ Ⓑ Ⓒ Ⓓ
22. Ⓕ Ⓖ Ⓗ Ⓙ
23. Ⓐ Ⓑ Ⓒ Ⓓ
24. Ⓕ Ⓖ Ⓗ Ⓙ
25. Ⓐ Ⓑ Ⓒ Ⓓ
26. Ⓕ Ⓖ Ⓗ Ⓙ
27. Ⓐ Ⓑ Ⓒ Ⓓ
28. Ⓐ Ⓑ Ⓒ Ⓓ
29. Ⓐ Ⓑ Ⓒ Ⓓ
30. Ⓐ Ⓑ Ⓒ Ⓓ

PRACTICE TEST TWO EXPLANATIONS

1. What is the volume of a cone with diameter 23 and height 40 (in cubic units)?

    A. 2,645π   B. 460π   C. 920π   D. 5,290π

2. In the figure, what is the value of X?

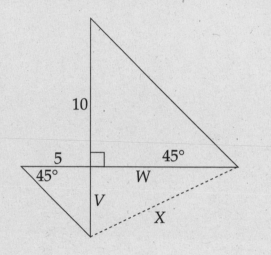

    A. $\sqrt{200}$

    B. $\sqrt{15}$

    C. $4\sqrt{50}$

    D. $\sqrt{125}$

A. is the correct answer. The volume of a cone = $1/2\pi r^2 h$. Plug in the numbers to find the volume.

Volume = $1/2\pi(11.5)^2(40) = 2645\pi$ cubic units

D. is the correct answer. Since the two legs of a 45° right triangle are congruent, you know that $W = 10$ and $V = 5$. Now you plug them in to the Pythagorean Theorem to find the hypotenuse.

$$\sqrt{(5^2 + 10)} = \sqrt{125}$$

3. Laura Anne cuts half of a pie into three equal pieces, and the other half into four equal pieces. If the area of one of the smaller pieces is $\pi 2$, what is the area of one of the larger pieces?

    A. $2\pi 3$

    B. $3\pi 8$

    C. π

    D. $1/8(\pi)$

A. is the correct answer. Each of the smaller pieces makes up 1/8 of the pie. The area for 1/8 of a circle is: $1/8 \, \pi r^2$. So, working backwards to find the radius:

$$\pi 2 = 1/8 \, \pi r^2 \qquad 4\pi = \pi r^2$$

$$4 = r^2 \qquad r = 2$$

Now, the area of one of the larger pieces is $1/6 \, \pi r^2$, so simply plug in the radius:

$$1/6 \, \pi(2)^2 = 2\pi 3$$

4. What is the perimeter of a regular decagon if one side is 24?

    A. 172   B. 240   C. 24   D. 2400

B. is the correct answer. A decagon has 10 sides. Therefore, 24 multiplied by 10 = 240.

5. If a cube with side 8 had the same volume as a sphere, what would the sphere's radius be, to the nearest tenth?

    A. 8.2   B. 5.0   C. 4.3   D. 2.4

B. is the correct answer. The volume of a cube $= s^3 = (8)^3 = 512$

The volume of a sphere $= 4/3 \, \pi r^3$

If they have the same volume, then $512 = 4/3 \, \pi r^3 \qquad r \approx 5.0$

6. In the figure, what is the measurement of ∠A?

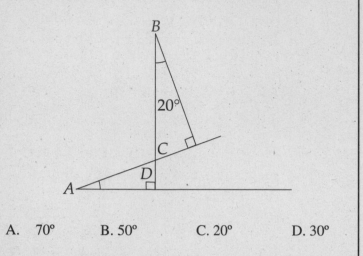

A. 70°   B. 50°   C. 20°   D. 30°

C.   is the correct answer. Since the angles of a triangle sum to 180°, we know that m∠C = 70°. ∠D is a vertical angle of ∠C, so it also equals 70°. To solve for the value of ∠A, once again use the knowledge that the sum of the angles in a triangle equals 180°. m∠A = 180° − 90° − 70°, or 20°.

7. If ray *a* bisects ∠*b*, and the measurement of ∠*c* is 110°, what is the measurement of ∠*d*?

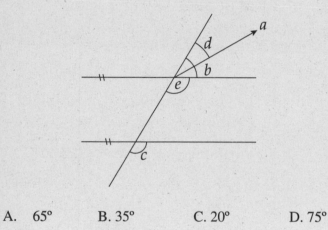

A. 65°   B. 35°   C. 20°   D. 75°

B.   is the correct answer. ∠*c* and ∠*e* are corresponding angles, and thus congruent. Therefore, ∠*e* = 110°. ∠*e* and ∠*b* are supplementary angles, so their sum is 180°. This means that m∠*b* = 180° − 110°, or 70°. ∠*d* is half of ∠*b*, so its measure is 35°.

8. In the figure, which side has length $16\sqrt{2}$?

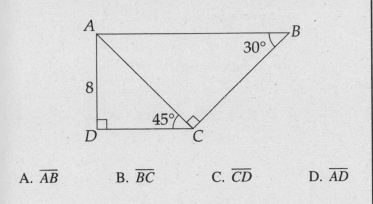

A. $\overline{AB}$ B. $\overline{BC}$ C. $\overline{CD}$ D. $\overline{AD}$

A. is the correct answer. The hypotenuse of a 45° right triangle is $\sqrt{2}$ × the length of the leg, so $AC = 8\sqrt{2}$. The hypotenuse of a 30-60-90 right triangle is twice the length of the side opposite the 30° angle, so $AB = 16\sqrt{2}$.

9. In triangle ABC, the measure of an exterior angle drawn at C is four times the measure of $\angle B$. If the measure of $\angle A = 33$, what is the measure of $\angle B$?

A. 40°   B. 132°   C. 147°   D. 11°

D. is the correct answer. An exterior angle in a triangle is equal to the sum of the other two angles, so:

$33 + B = 4B$
$B = 11$
$m\angle B = 11°$

10. In a store you see 2 cans of soup. Can A is 2 times as tall as Can B, and the radius of Can A is 1.3 times as large as Can B. How much more soup can be stored in Can A?

  A. 2.6 times more

  B. 3.4 times more

  C. 1.7 times more

  D. 3.3 times more

B. is the correct answer. The question is asking how much more volume Can A has than Can B.

Height Can A = 2 × (height Can B) $h_A = 2\,h_B$

Radius Can A = 1.3 × (radius Can B) $r_A = 1.3\,r_B$

First, remember that the volume of a cylinder is $\pi r^2 h$. Now find the volume of each can using the variables above.

Volume Can A = $\pi(1.3\,r_B)^2(2\,h_B) = 3.4\,\pi(r_B{}^2)(h_B)$

Volume Can B = $\pi(r_B{}^2)(h_B)$

As you can see, the volume of Can A is 3.4 times larger than the volume of Can B.

11. In the figure, if $\overline{EH}$ is a diameter of the circle, and it equals 42, and the length of the arc *EFG* is 33, then what is the measure of ∠*EFG*?

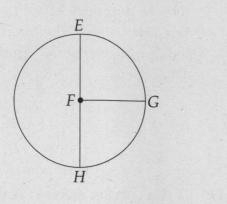

A. 90°   B. 42°   C. 84°   D. 73°

12. What is the measure of arc *x*?

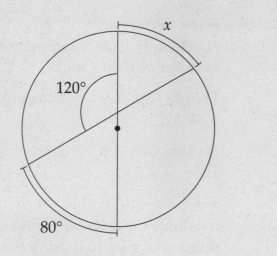

A. 40°   B. 60°   C. 80°   D. 120°

A. is the correct answer. The length of an arc = (angle/360) πd. Plug in the numbers given to find the angle.

33 = (angle/360) π(42)
measure of angle = 90°

A. is the correct answer. The angles that subtend *x* and the 80° arc are congruent, and equal to the average of 80° and *x*, or $\frac{1}{2}(80 + x)$.

Since each of these angles is also supplementary to the 120° angle, then:

$$\frac{1}{2}(80 + x) = 180 - 120$$

$$40 + \frac{1}{2}x = 60$$

$$\frac{1}{2}x = 20$$

$$x = 40$$

13. $\angle ABC$ measures 78°, and is bisected by *AD*. What is the measure of angle *ABD*?

A. 78°   B. 12°   C. 102°   D. 39°

14. In triangle ABC, the measure of $\angle A = 45$, measure of $\angle B = 30$ and $CB = 24$. What is *AC*?

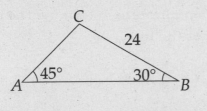

A. $12\sqrt{3}$ B. $24\sqrt{2}$ C. $12\sqrt{2}$ D. $12\sqrt{5}$

D. is the correct answer. An angle bisector divides an angle into two equal angles.

$$78/2 = 39$$

C. is the correct answer. Using the Law of Sines, you can easily determine the length of AC.

$\sin 45/24 = \sin 30/x$

$x \sin 45 = 24 \sin 30$

$x = (24 \sin 30)/\sin 45$

$x \approx 16.97$

16.97 is less than 24, so you can eliminate option B. Since all the remaining answers have a factor of 12, divide 16.97 by 12 and then square the quotient. This will give you approximately 2, letting you know that $12\sqrt{2}$ is the correct answer.

If you forget the Law of Sines, you can also solve this problem by drawing the altitude of the triangle, and using your knowledge of special right triangles.

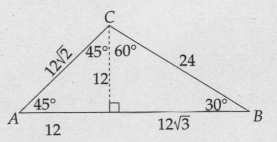

15. What is the equation of the line defined by the points (–7,–4) and (1,1)?

 A. $y = 5/8x + 5/8$

 B. $y = 5/8x + 3/8$

 C. $y = 3/8x + 5/8$

 D. $y = 3/8x + 3/8$

B. is the correct answer. Use the slope formula to determine the slope:

$$(-4 - 1)/(-7 - 1) = \frac{-5}{-8} = \frac{5}{8}$$

So, options C and D can be eliminated. Now, substitute one set of coordinates into the slope-intercept equation to determine the equation of the line.

$$y = \frac{5}{8}x + b$$

$$1 = \frac{5}{8}(1) + b$$

$$1 = \frac{5}{8} + b$$

$$b = \frac{3}{8}$$

$$y = \frac{5}{8}x + \frac{3}{8}$$

16. In the figure, triangle *ABC* and triangle *DEF* are similar triangles. What is the length of *x*?

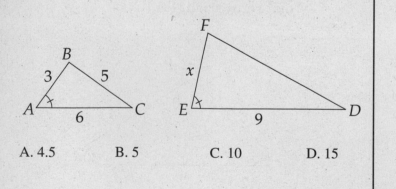

A. 4.5   B. 5   C. 10   D. 15

D. is the correct answer. Since they are similar triangles, it means that their corresponding sides are in proportion. So, we can set up the following equation to solve for *x*:

$x/5 = 9/3$

$x = 15$

17. In the figure, what is the area of the trapezoid (in square units)?

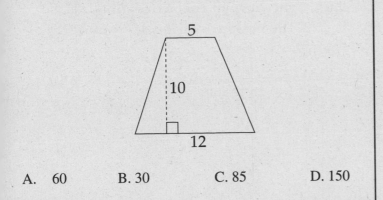

A. 60   B. 30   C. 85   D. 150

18. In the figure, *r* and *s* are parallel lines, cut by transversals *t*, *u*, and *v* (*v* is perpendicular to *r* and *s*). If ∠2 and ∠3 are congruent, which angle is congruent to ∠16?

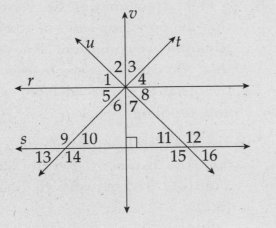

A. ∠2   B. ∠4   C. ∠6   D. ∠9

C. is the correct answer. The area of a trapezoid = $\frac{1}{2}(b_1 + b_2)h$. All the variables are given to you.

Area = $\frac{1}{2}(12 + 5)(10)$ = 85 square units

B. is the correct answer. Start finding angles that are congruent to ∠16 until you find one on the list of answers.

∠11 is a vertical angle to ∠16.

∠8 is an alternate interior angle to ∠11.

∠1 is a vertical angle to ∠8.

∠4 is a complement to an angle congruent to the complement of ∠1.

19. In the figure, what is the measure of ∠CAD?

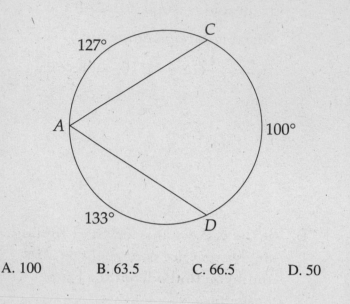

A. 100   B. 63.5   C. 66.5   D. 50

D. is the correct answer. The measure of an inscribed angle is half the measure of the arc it subtends, so the measure of ∠CAD is 50°.

20. What is the perimeter of the parallelogram in the figure?

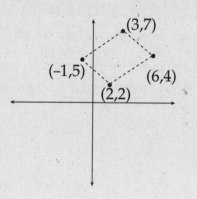

A. 17.43

B. 16

C. 18.29

D. 75.89

A. is the correct answer. Remember that the opposing sides of a parallelogram are congruent. Knowing this, you can save time by equating the distance of two adjacent sides, and doubling.

Use the distance formula to determine the distance between (2,2) and (6,4), and between (6,4) and (3,7):

$$\sqrt{(2 - 6^2) - (2 - 4^2)} = \sqrt{20}$$

$$\sqrt{(6 - 3^2) - (4 - 7^2)} = \sqrt{18}$$

$$2(\sqrt{20} + \sqrt{18}) = 4\sqrt{5} + 6\sqrt{2} \approx 17.43$$

21. What is the measure of ∠DAK?

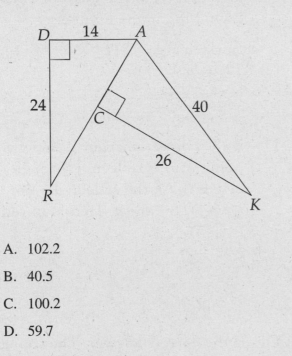

A. 102.2

B. 40.5

C. 100.2

D. 59.7

22. In triangles *ABC* and *DEF*, *BC* = *EF*, *AB* = *DE*, and m∠*B* = m∠*E*. Which of the following is used to show that *ABC* and *DEF* are congruent?

A. SSS   B. ASA   C. SSA   D. SAS

23. What is the area of a 50 degree sector if the radius of the circle is 4 (in square units)?

A. 32π   B. 2.2π   C. 0.32π   D. 8π

C.   is the correct answer. Use trigonometry to solve for the measures of ∠DAR and ∠ACK. Then, combine these values to get the measure of ∠DAK.

$$\tan \angle DAR = 24/14$$
$$\angle DAR = \tan^{-1}(24/14)$$

$$\angle DAR \approx 59.7$$

$$\sin \angle ACK = 26/40$$

$$\angle ACK = \sin^{-1}(26/40)$$

$$\angle ACK \approx 40.5$$

$$59.7 + 40.5 \approx 100.2$$

D.   is the correct answer. See the figure to observe the side-angle-side.

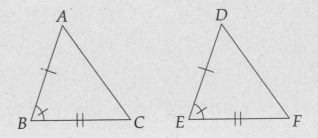

B.   is the correct answer. The area of the total circle is $\pi r^2 = 16\pi$.

But we only want 50° out of 360°, so we multiply $16\pi \times 50/360 \approx 2.2\pi$ square units.

24. If a rectangular box does not have a lid, what is its surface area if its length is 12, width is 5, and height is 14 (in square units)?

A. 840   B. 718   C. 421   D. 574

D. is the correct answer. The surface area of a rectangle is 2lw + 2lh + 2wh. Plug in the numbers.

Surface area = 2(14 × 5) + 3(14 × 12) = 574

25. What are the coordinates of the point (4,3) after being reflected about the origin?

   A. (–3,–4)

   B. (–4,3)

   C. (3,–4)

   D. (–4,–3)

D. is the correct answer. Whenever a point (x,y) is reflected through the origin (0,0), the reflected point is $(-x,-y)$. So, the reflection of (4,3) is (–4,–3).

26. How many triangles are shown in this figure?

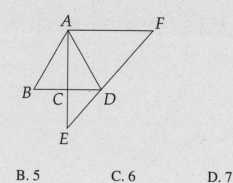

A. 4   B. 5   C. 6   D. 7

D. is the correct answer. The triangles are: *ABC, ACD, ABD, ADF, CDE, AEF, ADE*

27. If a regular polygon has 10 sides, what is the degree measure of each angle?

A. 180   B. 90   C. 144   D. 162

C. is the correct answer. Use the following equation to solve this problem:

angle measurement = $180 (n - 2)/n$

angle measurement = $180 (10 - 2)/10 = 144$

28. In the figure, what is the perimeter of the rhombus?

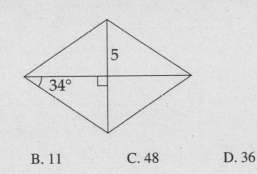

A. 17   B. 11   C. 48   D. 36

D.   is the correct answer. First off, rule out obviously wrong answers. Remember that the diagonals of a rhombus meet at a right angle. This means that the line that measures 5 is a leg of a right triangle whose hypotenuse is the length of a side of the rhombus. Since a hypotenuse of a right triangle is always longer than each of its legs, the side of the rhombus must be longer than 5, and the perimeter must be longer than 20 (4 × side). So, A and B are incorrect answers.

Now, set up a triangle on which you can use trigonometry to solve for the hypotenuse. Remember that the diagonals of a rhombus bisect each other, and that the angles of a triangle sum to 180°, and you can set up the following triangle:

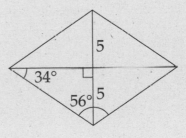

Now, you can use trigonometry to solve for the length of the hypotenuse:

sin 34 = 5/hypotenuse

(hypotenuse)sin 34 = 5

hypotenuse = 5/(sin 34)

hypotenuse ≈ 8.94

perimeter = 4 × 8.94 ≈ 35.7, which is approximately 36.

29. How much liquid can be contained in a cylindrical pan if the surface area of the pen is 48π and the diameter is 8 (in cubed units)?

A. 32π B. 16π C. 64π D. 24π

A. is the correct answer. The question is asking for volume of the cylinder. The equation for volume is $\pi r^2 h$. You are given the radius (half the diameter) in the question, but you are not given the height. So, you must find the height using the equation for surface area, since they give you surface area.

Surface area $= 2\pi r^2 + \pi \partial h = 2\pi(4)^2 + \pi(8)h = 48\pi$

$h = 2$

Now, you can use $h = 2$ to find the volume.

Volume $= \pi r^2 h = \pi(4)^2(2) = 32\pi$ cubed units

30. In the figure, $\triangle LMN$ has been dilated by a factor of 3. If the coordinates of M are $(4,1)$, what are the coordinates of M'?

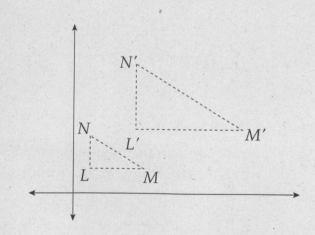

A. (3,12)

B. (12,3)

C. (1,4)

D. (10,2)

B. is the correct answer. To perform a dilation, simply multiply the original coordinates by the dilation factor to compute the coordinates of the dilated image.

TEST TWO, DAY TWO

1. In the figure, ray *BC* bisects ∠*ABD*. What is the measure of ∠*ABD*?

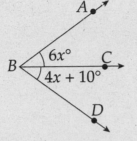

The correct answer is 60°. Since BC bisects ∠*ABD*, you know that m∠*ABC* = m∠*CBD*, or

$6x = 4x + 10$ solve for x

$2x = 10$

$x = 5$ plug $x = 5$ back in

m∠*ABD* = $6x + 4x + 10 = 6(5) + 4(5) + 10 = 30 + 20 + 10 = 60°$

2. In the figure, what is the value of *x* to the nearest tenth?

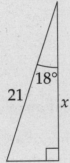

20.0 is the correct answer. Cos 18° $= x/21$; $x ≈ 20.0$

3. In the figure, what is the area of the rhombus, in square units?

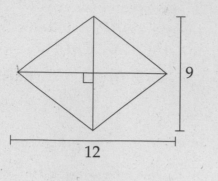

54 is the correct answer. The formula for the area of a rhombus is: $\frac{1}{2}(\partial_1 \times \partial_2)$ So, the area of this rhombus is:

$1/2\ (9 \times 12) = 54$ square units

4. If a regular polygon has 12 sides, what is the degree measure of each of its angles?

The correct answer is 150. Use the equation degree measure = $180 (n-2)/n$, where n = # sides

degree measure = $180\ (12-2)/12 = 1{,}800/12 = 150$

5. What is the volume of the shaded area to the nearest tenth, if the inner cylinder's radius is 4 and the outer cylinder's radius is 6 (in cubed units)?

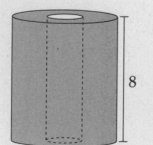

The correct answer is 502.7.

The volume of a cylinder is $\pi r^2 h$. For this problem, take the volume of the smaller cylinder and subtract it from the volume of the larger cylinder to find the shaded volume.

Shaded volume = $\pi\ (6)^2(8) - \pi\ (4)^2(8) = 288\pi - 128\pi = 160\pi = 502.7$ cubed units

Written Response Question

1. The vertices of the base of a regular pentagon are located at (1,1) and (4,1) on a Cartesian plane. Explain how to find the coordinates of the other three vertices. Specify each idea you use.

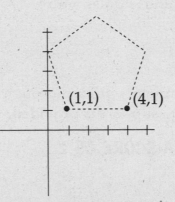

Remember to show all parts of your solution, and explain how you arrived at your answer.

SAMPLE RESPONSE RECEIVING A SCORE OF 4

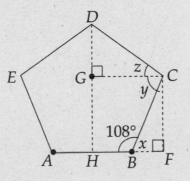

Each side of a regular polygon is congruent, so each side is 3 units long.

Each angle of a regular pentagon is 108° ($1/n \times (n-2) (180)$)

$\angle x = 72°$ (Supplementary angles sum to 180°, and 180° − 108° = 72°)

$BF = 3 \times \cos 72$ (adjacent = hypotenuse times cos x)

$BF = .927$ (simplification)

$CF = 3 \times \sin 72$ (opposite = hypotenuse times sin x)

$CF = 2.85$ (simplification)

$C = (4 + .927, 1 + 2.85)$

$C = (4.93, 3.85)$

$E = (1 − .927, 1 + 2.85)$ (regular pentagons are symmetrical)

$E = (.07, 3.85)$

$\angle y = 72°$ (The angles in a quadrilateral sum to 360°. For quad. $BCGH$, $-y = 360° - 90° - 90° - 108°$)
$\angle z = 36°$ ($\angle z = 108° - 72°$)
$CG = 3 \times \cos 36$ (adjacent = hypotenuse times $\cos x$)
$CG = 2.43$ (simplification)
$DG = 3 \times \sin 36$ (opposite = hypotenuse times $\sin x$)
$DG = 1.76$ (simplification)
$D = (4.93 - 2.43, 3.85 + 1.76)$
$D = (2.5, 5.61)$

This response is accurate and complete, with a thorough explanation. The supporting diagram is well labeled, and necessary support is provided, with accurate terminology.

SAMPLE RESPONSE RECEIVING A SCORE OF 2

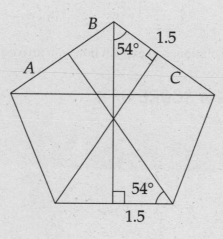

tan 54 = opp/1.5
opp = 2.06
cos 54 = 1.5/hyp
hyp = 2.55
$B = (2.5, 5.61)$
Congruent triangles, so:
$A = (2.5 - 2.06, 5.61 - 1.5)$
$A = (.44, 4.11)$
$C = (2.5 + 2.06, 5.61 - 1.5)$
$C = (4.56, 4.11)$

This response lacks explanation, but it does demonstrate some knowledge of regular polygons, right triangles, and coordinate geometry. The error made in determining that the triangle with a hypotenuse of AB is congruent with the triangle at the bottom of the diagram limits this response to two points. The two triangles are similar, not congruent, so the calculation results in an error.

Chapter 15

PRACTICE
TEST THREE

SAMPLE MULTIPLE-CHOICE QUESTIONS FOR GEOMETRY

Make sure you have two or three No. 2 pencils with erasers and a ruler or straightedge available to you during the exam. You also may have a calculator; it may be either a scientific or graphing calculator. You may not use minicomputers, pocket organizers, or calculators with QWERTY (typewriter) keyboards. You may not share your calculator with other students.

Do not spend too much time on a question that seems too difficult. Answer the easier questions first and then return to the harder ones if you have the time. Try to answer every question, even if you have to guess.

Notes: (1) Figures that accompany problems are drawn as accurately as possible EXCEPT when it is stated that a figure is not drawn to scale. All figures lie in a plane unless otherwise indicated.

(2) All numbers used are real numbers. All algebraic expressions represent real numbers unless otherwise indicated.

TEST THREE, DAY ONE

1. In the triangle, what is the value of z?

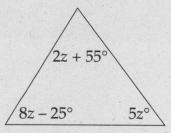

Note: Figure not drawn to scale.

A. 10   B. 4.6   C. 16.5   D. 20

2. What is the area of a square whose opposite corners are (1,3) and (6,4)?

A. 13 square units

B. 26 square units

C. 139 square units

D. 10 square units

3. What is the area of this isosceles triangle?

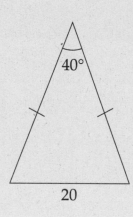

Note: Figure not drawn to scale.

A. 549 square units

B. 275 square units

C. 31 square units

D. 965 square units

4. If a gallon of paint can cover 45 square units, how many gallons will be needed to cover the walls of a house with dimensions as indicated in the figure?

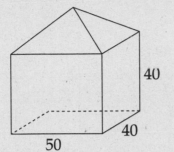

40

40

50

Note: Figure not drawn to scale.

A. 72   B. 45   C. 160   D. 80

5. What is the midpoint of the line segment with endpoints (−3,6) and (5,−2)?

A. (1,1)   B. (2,2)   C. (1,2)   D. (2,1)

6. What is the area of a rhombus with base 4 and height 5 (in square units)?

A. 20   B. 10   C. 40   D. 18

7. What is the length of diameter $\overline{QR}$?

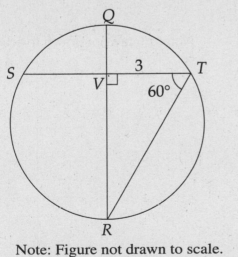

Note: Figure not drawn to scale.

A. $3/\sqrt{3}$ B. $3\sqrt{3}$ C. $12/\sqrt{3}$ D. 3

8. In the triangle, what is the value of z?

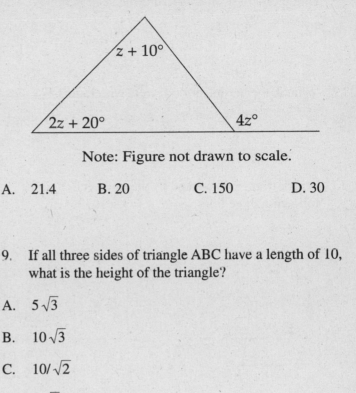

Note: Figure not drawn to scale.

A. 21.4   B. 20   C. 150   D. 30

9. If all three sides of triangle ABC have a length of 10, what is the height of the triangle?

A. $5\sqrt{3}$

B. $10\sqrt{3}$

C. $10/\sqrt{2}$

D. $5\sqrt{2}$

10. In the figure, what is the measurement of x?

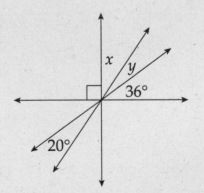

Note: Figure not drawn to scale.

A. 70°   B. 36°   C. 124°   D. 34°

11. What is the surface area of a pyramid if 12 is the length of a base side and 10 is the slant height?

A. 240   B. 144   C. 120   D. 384

12. What is the perimeter of a circle with radius 12?

A. 12π B. 24π C. 6π D. 36π

13. Which triangle is created by the intersection of the following three lines: $y = x$; $y = 3$; $x = 7$?

A.

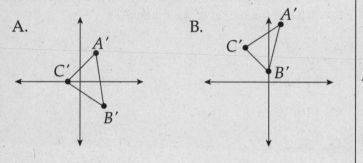

B.

C.

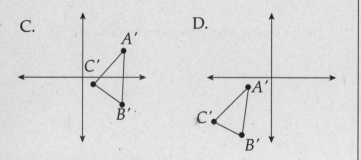

D.

Note: Figure not drawn to scale.

14. In the figure, what is the measure of major arc CD?

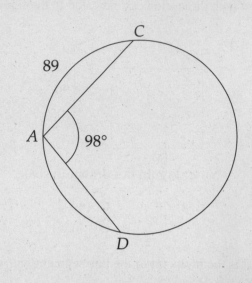

Note: Figure not drawn to scale.

A. 196   B. 89   C. 75   D. 98

15. In the figure, what can be used to prove that triangle ABC is congruent to triangle CDE?

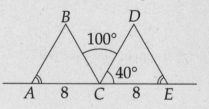

Note: Figure not drawn to scale.

A. SSS   B. SSA   C. ASA   D. AAA

16. In the triangle, what is *AB* to the nearest tenth?

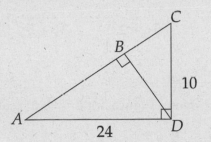

Note: Figure not drawn to scale.

A. 26　　　　B. 22.6　　　　C. 24　　　　D. 22.2

17. ∠*a* and ∠*b* are supplementary. ∠*b* and ∠*c* are complementary. The measure of ∠*a* is 110°. What is the measure of ∠*c*?

A.　110°　　　B. 70°　　　　C. 20°　　　　D. 130°

18. In the figure, what is the perimeter of the triangle?

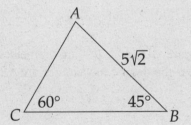

Note: Figure not drawn to scale.

A.　$5 + 5\sqrt{3} + 10\sqrt{2}$

B.　$10 + 10/\sqrt{2} + 10/\sqrt{3}$

C.　$5 + 10\sqrt{2} + 15/\sqrt{3}$

D.　$5 + 5\sqrt{2} + 15/\sqrt{3}$

19. If a solid sphere of diameter 20 is placed in a square box of height 25, how much empty space is there in the box (in cubed units)?

A.　11,437

B.　15,625

C.　4,188

D.　225

20. In the figure, what is the area of the regular pentagon (in square units)?

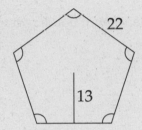

Note: Figure not drawn to scale.

A. 572　　　　B. 1,430　　　　C. 286　　　　D. 715

21. In the figure, the line P' is the line P reflected by the x-axis. If the equation for the line P is $y = 3x + 2$, what is the equation for the line P'?

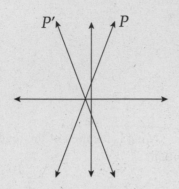

Note: Figure not drawn to scale.

A. $y = -3x - 2$

B. $y = -(1/3)x - 2$

C. $y = (1/3)x - 2$

D. $y = -3x + 2$

22. Which of these three triangles in the figure can be proven to be congruent because of the AAS Congruence Theorem?

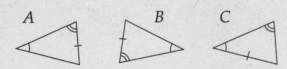

Note: Figure not drawn to scale.

A. all three

B. A and B

C. B and C

D. A and C

23. In the parallelogram shown below, what is the measure of $\angle a$?

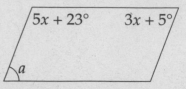

Note: Figure not drawn to scale.

A. 118°　　　B. 62°　　　C. 41°　　　D. 26°

24. In the figure, what is the length of b?

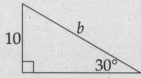

Note: Figure not drawn to scale.

A. $10\sqrt{3}$

B. 5

C. $10/\sqrt{3}$

D. 20

25. In the figure, $\overline{AD}$ and $\overline{EC}$ are diameters of the circle O. What is the degree measure of arc AB?

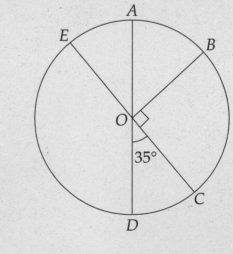

Note: Figure not drawn to scale.

A. 90　　　B. 35　　　C. 55　　　D. 145

26. In the figure, the sum of m∠a and m∠b is 60°. What is the measure of ∠c?

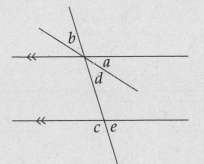

Note: Figure not drawn to scale.

A. 60°   B. 120°   C. 30°   D. 90°

27. If a cylinder of radius 5 has volume of 125, what is its height?

A. 5/π   B. 5π   C. 25π   D. 0.5π

28. What is the area of the figure (in square units)?

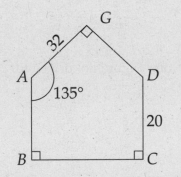

Note: Figure not drawn to scale.

A. $512 + 640\sqrt{2}$

B. $640\sqrt{2}$

C. $1{,}152\sqrt{2}$

D. 1,424

29. In the figure, △RST has been dilated by a factor of 2. If the coordinates of R are (–1,–4), what are the coordinates of R´?

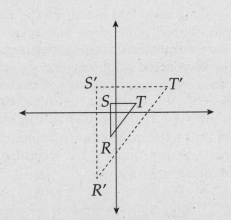

Note: Figure not drawn to scale.

A. (–3,–12)

B. (–12,–3)

C. (–1,–4)

D. (–2,–8)

30. The figure shows three regular pentagons. What is the sum of angles x, y, and z?

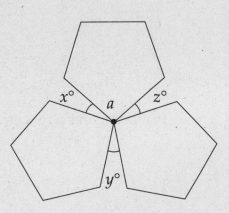

Note: Figure not drawn to scale.

A. 120   B. 36   C. 90   D. 18

SAMPLE GRIDDED-RESPONSE QUESTIONS FOR GEOMETRY

The following questions are similar to the multiple-choice questions, but answer choices are not provided. You must determine the answers yourself using separate scratch paper, and then use a special area on the answer sheet like the one shown here to bubble in your answers. If the answer is a mixed numeral, it is to be gridded as a decimal or improper fraction (e.g., 3 1/2 should be gridded as 7/2 or 3.5).

Grid your response to items #1 through #5 below. Use the decimal (.) or the fraction sign (/) if your answers require it.

Examples of how to grid your answers

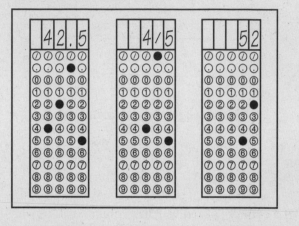

TEST THREE, DAY TWO

1. In the figure, $\overline{EB}$ is parallel to $\overline{DC}$. What is the value of $x + y$?

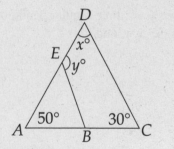

Note: Figure not drawn to scale.

2. What is the value of $\angle x$ to the nearest tenth?

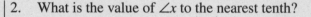
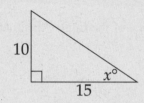

10

15

Note: Figure not drawn to scale.

3. What is the area of the isosceles trapezoid in the figure (in square units)?

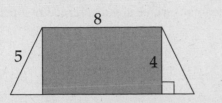

Note: Figure not drawn to scale.

4. What is the perimeter of a rectangle created by the x-axis, y-axis, and the point (–7,4)?

(–7,4)

Note: Figure not drawn to scale.

5. What is the volume (in square units) of a square building of side 12 with a pyramid roof with a slant height of 14 (to the nearest whole unit)?

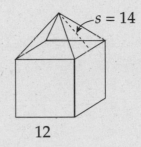

Note: Figure not drawn to scale.

Written Response Question

1. You open the can of soda in the figure below. By what percent is the total surface area decreased by opening it?

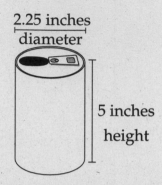

2.25 inches
diameter

5 inches
height

Note: Figure not drawn to scale.

height = 5 inches

diameter = 2.25 inches

diameter of circular opening = .75 inches

Remember to show all parts of your solution, and explain how you arrived at your answer.

ANSWER KEY TO GEOMETRY PRACTICE TEST THREE

Day One Questions:

Day Two Questions:

1 A	
2 A	
3 B	
4 C	
5 C	
6 A	
7 C	
8 D	
9 A	
10 D	
11 D	
12 B	
13 B	
14 A	
15 C	
16 D	
17 C	
18 D	
19 A	
20 D	
21 A	
22 B	
23 B	
24 D	
25 C	
26 B	
27 A	
28 A	
29 D	
30 B	

Grid-Ins:

1 180

2 33.7

3 44

4 22

5 2,335

Written Response:

1 See explanations for a properly credited response.

GRID-IN ANSWER SHEET

1

2

3

4

5

6

7

8

9

10

1

YOUR NAME: _____
(Print)   Last   First   M.I.

SIGNATURE: _____ **DATE:** ___/___/___

HOME ADDRESS: _____
(Print)   Number and Street

_____
City   State   Zip Code

PHONE NO.: _____
(Print)

Completely darken bubbles with a No. 2 pencil. If you make a mistake, be sure to erase mark completely. Erase all stray marks.

Practice Test Three

1. (A) (B) (C) (D)
2. (F) (G) (H) (J)
3. (A) (B) (C) (D)
4. (F) (G) (H) (J)
5. (A) (B) (C) (D)
6. (F) (G) (H) (J)
7. (A) (B) (C) (D)
8. (F) (G) (H) (J)
9. (A) (B) (C) (D)
10. (F) (G) (H) (J)
11. (A) (B) (C) (D)
12. (F) (G) (H) (J)
13. (A) (B) (C) (D)
14. (F) (G) (H) (J)
15. (A) (B) (C) (D)

16. (F) (G) (H) (J)
17. (A) (B) (C) (D)
18. (F) (G) (H) (J)
19. (A) (B) (C) (D)
20. (F) (G) (H) (J)
21. (A) (B) (C) (D)
22. (F) (G) (H) (J)
23. (A) (B) (C) (D)
24. (F) (G) (H) (J)
25. (A) (B) (C) (D)
26. (F) (G) (H) (J)
27. (A) (B) (C) (D)
28. (A) (B) (C) (D)
29. (A) (B) (C) (D)
30. (A) (B) (C) (D)

PRACTICE TEST THREE
EXPLANATIONS

1. In the triangle, what is the value of z?

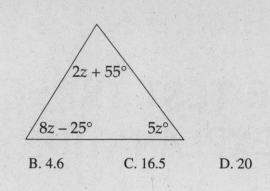

A. 10   B. 4.6   C. 16.5   D. 20

A. is the correct answer. In a triangle, the three angles must add up to 180°. Therefore,

$$2z + 55 + 8z - 25 + 5z = 18$$
$$15z + 30 = 180$$
$$15z = 150$$
$$z = 10$$

2. What is the area of a square whose opposite corners are (1,3) and (6,4)?

   A. 13 square units

   B. 26 square units

   C. 139 square units

   D. 10 square units

A. is the correct answer. There are a number of ways to approach this problem. The easiest way to solve this one is to realize that the line between the given points (1,3) and (6,4) is the square's **diagonal**, and that the area of a square can be calculated by taking half of the square of the diagonal (1/2 d^2).

So, first, use the distance formula to solve for the length of the diagonal, and then use the formula for area.

$$\sqrt{(1-6)^2 + (3-4)^2}$$

Distance = $\sqrt{26}$

Area = 1/2 $(\sqrt{26})^2$

Area = 13 square units

In case the only formula you remember for the area of a square is side squared (s^2), then you can figure out the length of a side of the square using the distance formula and the Pythagorean Theorem. As we discovered above, the distance of the diagonal is $\sqrt{26}$. Now, notice that the diagonal is the hypotenuse of a 45° right triangle, with two sides of the square for legs. Since the leg of a 45° right triangle equals (hypotenuse/$\sqrt{2}$), the length of a side is $\sqrt{13}$. Now, using area = s^2, it is easy to see that the area of the square is 13 square units.

3. What is the area of this isosceles triangle?

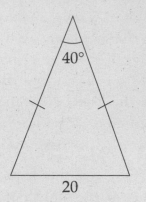

40°

20

A. 549 square units

B. 275 square units

C. 31 square units

D. 965 square units

B. is the correct answer. First, draw a height for the triangle. Because this is an isosceles triangle, this line bisects the 40° angle, and it bisects the opposite side into two equal segments. Now, use trigonometry to solve for the length of the height:

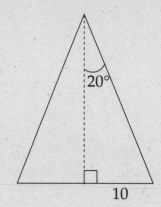

20°

10

$\tan 20 = 10/\text{adjacent}$

$(\text{adjacent})\tan 20 = 10$

$\text{adjacent} = 10/(\tan 20)$

$\text{adjacent} \approx 27.47$

area of a triangle $= 1/2(bh)$

$\text{area} = 1/2 (20 \times 27.47)$

$\text{area} \approx 274.7$

Rounded to the nearest whole number, the area is 275 square units.

4. If a gallon of paint can cover 45 square units, how many gallons will be needed to cover the walls of a house with dimensions as indicated in the figure?

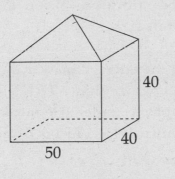

A. 72   B. 45   C. 160   D. 80

C. is the correct answer. You only need enough paint to cover the four sides of the house. You are given the lengths of the sides.

Front of house = 50 × 40 = 2,000
Back of house = 50 × 40 = 2,000

Side of house = 40 × 40 = 1,600
Side of house = 40 × 40 = 1,600

Total sides of house = 2,000 + 2,000 + 1,600 + 1,600 = 7,200 square units.

Since each gallon can cover 45 square units, simply divide 7,200 by 45 = 160.

5. What is the midpoint of the line segment with endpoints (–3,6) and (5,–2)?

A. (1,1)   B. (2,2)   C. (1,2)   D. (2,1)

C. is the correct answer. In order to solve this problem, simply utilize the midpoint formula, taking the average of the x-coordinates and the average of the y-coordinates.

$$\text{Midpoint} = \left(\frac{-3+5}{2}\right), \left(\frac{6+-2}{2}\right) =$$

$$\frac{2}{2}, \left(\frac{4}{2}\right) = (1,2)$$

6. What is the area of a rhombus with base 4 and height 5 (in square units)?

A. 20   B. 10   C. 40   D. 18

7. What is the length of diameter $\overline{QR}$?

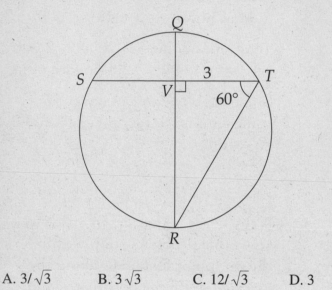

A. $3/\sqrt{3}$ B. $3\sqrt{3}$ C. $12/\sqrt{3}$ D. 3

8. In the triangle, what is the value of z?

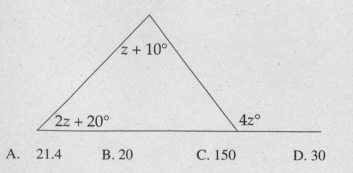

A. 21.4   B. 20   C. 150   D. 30

A. is the correct answer. The equation for the area of a rhombus = base × height, which you are given. Therefore, the area = 4 × 5 = 20 square units.

C. is the correct answer. First off, recognize that $\triangle TRV$ is a 30-60-90 right triangle. The measure of the shortest leg (TV) is 3 and the longer leg (VR) is $3\sqrt{3}$.

Next, remember that when the diameter of a circle intersects another chord at a right angle, it bisects it. So, SV and VT are both 3 units in length.

Next, remember that when two chords intersect in a circle, the products of their segments are equal, so:

$QV \times VR = SV \times VT$

$QV \times 3\sqrt{3} = 3 \times 3$

$3\sqrt{3}\, QV = 9$

$QV = 3/\sqrt{3}$

$QR = 3\sqrt{3} + 3/\sqrt{3} = \dfrac{12}{\sqrt{3}}$

D. is the correct answer. Set up an equation using the rule that the external angle of a triangle equals the sum of the other two angles:

$(z + 10) + (2z + 20) = 4z$

$3z + 30 = 4z$

$z = 30$

9. If all three sides of triangle ABC have a length of 10, what is the height of the triangle?

A. $5\sqrt{3}$

B. $10\sqrt{3}$

C. $10/\sqrt{2}$

D. $5\sqrt{2}$

A. is the correct answer. A triangle with three equal sides is an equilateral triangle. The height of the triangle divides the base into two equal segments, creating two 30-60-90 right triangles.

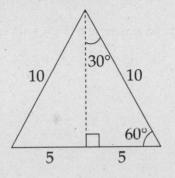

Remember that the side opposite the 60° angle is the length of the shortest side multiplied by $\sqrt{3}$. So, the length of the height is $5\sqrt{3}$.

10. In the figure, what is the measurement of *x*?

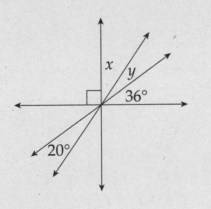

A. 70°   B. 36°   C. 124°   D. 34°

D. is the correct answer. ∠y is a vertical angle to the 20° angle, so it is also 20°. The values of the 36° angle and ∠y can be combined to form a 56° angle, which is complementary to ∠x. Therefore, m ∠x = 90° − 56°, or 34°.

11. What is the surface area of a pyramid if 12 is the length of a base side and 10 is the slant height (in square units)?

A. 240   B. 144   C. 120   D. 384

D. is the correct answer. The surface area of a pyramid is $a^2 + 4(1/2)as$. You are given all the variables.

$$SA = (12)^2 + 2(12)(10) = 144 + 240 = 384 \text{ square units.}$$

12. What is the perimeter of a circle with radius 12?

A. 12π B. 24π C. 6π D. 36π

B. is the correct answer. The perimeter of a circle is called the circumference. The circumference of a circle = $2\pi r$. You are given the radius, and so you can simply plug it in. The perimeter = $2\pi r = 2\pi(12) = 24\pi$.

13. Which triangle is created by the intersection of the following three lines: $y = x$; $y = 3$; $x = 7$?

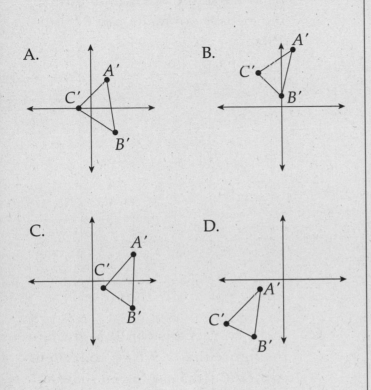

A.

B.

C.

D.

B. is the correct answer. By drawing the graphs of each of these lines, you can determine what the triangle will look like, and where it will be located on the coordinate plane.

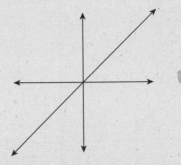

After drawing the graph of $y = x$, you can eliminate choices A and C.

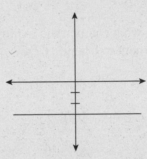

After drawing the graph of $y = 3$, you can eliminate choice D, leaving B as the correct answer.

14. In the figure, what is the measure of major arc CD?

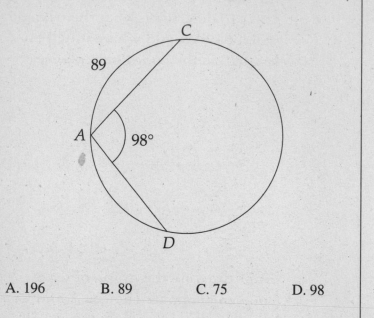

A. 196   B. 89   C. 75   D. 98

A. is the correct answer. The measure of an inscribed angle is half the measure of the arc it subtends, so the measure of major arc *CD* is 196°.

15. In the figure, what can be used to prove that triangle *ABC* is congruent to triangle *CDE*?

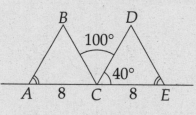

A. SSS   B. SSA   C. ASA   D. AAA

C. is the correct answer. It is given in the figure that ∠*BAC* is congruent to ∠*DEC*. It is also given that both *AC* and *CE* = 8. Finally, you can determine that m∠*BCA* = 40°, because 180 − 100 − 40 = 40. Therefore, you know that m∠*DCE* = m∠*BCA*. Angle-side-angle.

16. In the triangle, what is *AB* to the nearest tenth?

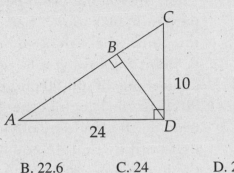

A. 26   B. 22.6   C. 24   D. 22.2

D. is the correct answer. First off, use the Pythagorean Theorem to solve for the length of *AC*:

$$AC^2 = 24^2 + 10^2$$

$$AC^2 = 576 + 100$$

$$AC^2 = 676$$

$$AC = 26$$

We can now use trigonometry to solve for *AB*.

$$\cos \angle A = 24/26$$

$$\angle A = \cos^{-1}(24/26)$$

$$m\angle A \approx 22.6°$$

$$\cos 22.6 = AB/24$$

$$24\ (\cos 22.6) = AB$$

$$AB \approx 22.2$$

17. $\angle a$ and $\angle b$ are supplementary. $\angle b$ and $\angle c$ are complementary. The measure of $\angle a$ is 110°. What is the measure $\angle c$?

A. 110°   B. 70°   C. 20°   D. 130°

C. is the correct answer. You can rewrite the question as follows:

$$m\angle a + m\angle b = 180°$$
$$m\angle b + m\angle c = 90°$$

If $m\angle a = 110°$, then $m\angle b = 70°$.
If $m\angle b = 70°$, then $m\angle c = 20°$.

18. In the figure, what is the perimeter of the triangle?

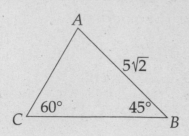

A. $5 + 5\sqrt{3} + 10\sqrt{2}$

B. $10 + 10/\sqrt{2} + 10/\sqrt{3}$

C. $5 + 10\sqrt{2} + 15/\sqrt{3}$

D. $5 + 5\sqrt{2} + 15/\sqrt{3}$

D. is the correct answer.

First, draw a line from point A perpendicular to BC. Let's say that the point where the two lines meet is point E. Now, you have two right angles: one 30-60-90 and one 45-45-90. First, let's look at the 45-45-90 triangle. It should be obvious to you that both EB and AE equal 5, since the hypotenuse of a 45-45-90 triangle equals one side times $\sqrt{2}$. Already, you have half the perimeter of the total triangle ($5\sqrt{2} + 5$). Next, look at the 30-60-90 triangle. You already learned that $AE = 5$. Therefore, CE must equal $5/\sqrt{3}$, and then AC equals $10/\sqrt{3}$. That gives you the rest of the perimeter.

The perimeter equals $AB + EB + CE + CA = 5\sqrt{2} + 5 + 5/\sqrt{3} + 10/\sqrt{3} = 5\sqrt{2} + 5 + 15/\sqrt{3}$.

19. If a solid sphere of diameter 20 is placed in a square box of height 25, how much empty space is there in the box (in cubed units)?

A. 11,437

B. 15,625

C. 4,188

D. 225

A. is the correct answer. For this question, you need to calculate the volume of a sphere and subtract that from the volume of a cube.

Volume of a sphere $= (4/3)\pi r^3 = (4/3)\pi 10^3 = 1,333\pi \approx 4,188$

Volume of a cube $= s^3 = 25^3 = 15,625$

Volume cube − volume sphere = volume empty space $= 15,625 - 4,188 \approx 11,437$ cubed units

20. In the figure, what is the area of the regular pentagon (in squared units)?

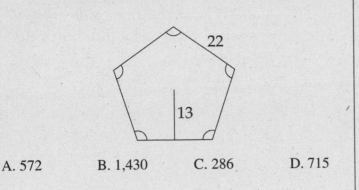

A. 572   B. 1,430   C. 286   D. 715

21. In the figure, the line P' is the line P reflected by the x-axis. If the equation for the line P is $y = 3x + 2$, what is the equation for the line P'?

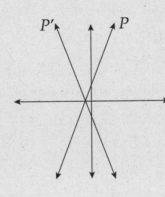

A. $y = -3x - 2$

B. $y = -(1/3)x - 2$

C. $y = (1/3)x - 2$

D. $y = -3x + 2$

D. is the correct answer. The area of a regular pentagon is $\frac{1}{2}$ (apothem × perimeter). Remember, the apothem is the distance from the center of the polygon perpendicular to one side. In the figure, we are given the apothem and the length of one side. The perimeter = 22 × 5 = 110. Then plug in the numbers to find area.

Area = $\frac{1}{2}$ (13 × 110) = 715 squared units

A. is the correct answer. When a line is reflected about the x-axis or y-axis, the sign of the slope is changed. A slope of 3 becomes –3 when re-flected about the x-axis (or y-axis, for that matter). Now, you need to determine the y-intercept. Remember that when a point is reflected about the x-axis, the x-coordinate remains the same (in this case, 0), and the y-coordinate changes signs (so 2 becomes –2).

So, the equation of P' is $y = -3x - 2$. You can double-check the equation by finding any point on P, changing the sign of the y coordinate, and plugging the coordinates into the equation for P'.

22. Which of these three triangles in the figure can be proven to be congruent because of the AAS Congruence Theorem?

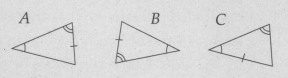

A. all three

B. *A* and *B*

C. *B* and *C*

D. *A* and *C*

B. is the correct answer. They all have the same two angles congruent, but *A* and *B* have the same side congruent, whereas *C* has a different side congruent.

23. In the parallelogram shown below, what is the measure of $\angle a$?

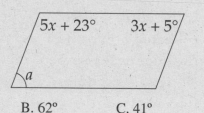

A. 118°   B. 62°   C. 41°   D. 26°

B. is the correct answer. Any two adjacent angles of a parallelogram sums to 180°, so you can set up the following equation:

$(5x + 23) + (3x + 5) = 180$

$8x + 28 = 180$

$x = 19$

Since opposing angles of a parallelogram are congruent, then
m$\angle a = 3x + 5$

m$\angle a = 3(19) + 5$

m$\angle a = 62°$

24. In the figure, what is the length of *b*?

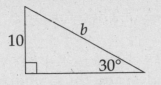

A. $10\sqrt{3}$

B. 5

C. $10/\sqrt{3}$

D. 20

D. is the correct answer. In a 30-60-90 triangle, the side whose opposite angle is 30° = 1/2 the length of the hypotenuse. If that side is 10, then the hypotenuse is 20.

25. In the figure, $\overline{AD}$ and $\overline{EC}$ are diameters of the circle *O*. What is the degree measure of arc *AB*?

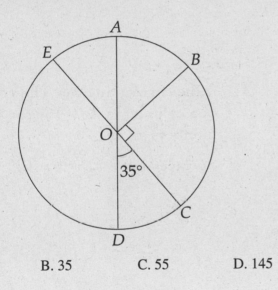

A. 90   B. 35   C. 55   D. 145

C. is the correct answer. Diameters intersect at the center of a circle, so $\angle DOC$ is a central angle, and thus has the same measure as the arc it subtends, 35°. $\angle EOA$ is a vertical angle to $\angle DOC$, so it is also 35°. Since $\angle BOC$ is a right angle, then $\angle EOB$ is also a right angle, which means that $\angle EOA$ and $\angle AOB$ are complementary. $\angle AOB$, then is 55°, and the arc it subtends, *AB*, is also 55°.

26. In the figure, the sum of m∠a and m∠b is 60°. What is the measure of ∠c?

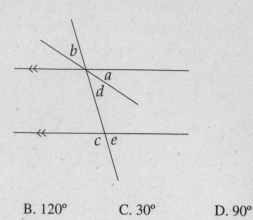

A. 60°   B. 120°   C. 30°   D. 90°

B. is the correct answer. ∠b and ∠∂ are vertical angles, and thus congruent. Therefore m∠∂ + m∠a = 60°.
∠∂ + ∠a and ∠e are corresponding angles, and thus congruent. Therefore, m∠e = 60°. ∠e and ∠c are supplementary angles, and thus m∠ c = 180° − m∠e. Therefore, m∠c = 120°.

27. If a cylinder of radius 5 has a volume of 125, what is its height?

A. 5/π   B. 5π   C. 25π   D. 0.5π

A. is the correct answer. The volume of a cylinder is $\pi r^2 h$. Plug in the numbers given.

Surface area = $\pi(5)^2 h = 125$.

$h = 5/\pi$

28. What is the area of the figure (in square units)?

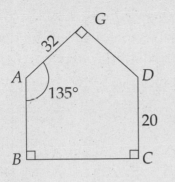

A. $512 + 640\sqrt{2}$

B. $640\sqrt{2}$

C. $1152\sqrt{2}$

D. 1424

A. is the correct answer. You can easily solve this problem if you draw a line from A to D so that you have a triangle on top and a rectangle on the bottom. First, find the area of the triangle. The original degree measure $\angle A$ is 135. Once you draw the line, in order to find the degree measure of $\angle GAD$, simply subtract 90. The degree measure of $\angle GAD$ is 45°. Since this is a special triangle, and you know that the side AG is 32, you now know that AD (which is both the hypotenuse of the triangle and a side of the rectangle) is $32\sqrt{2}$. You can then easily calculate the area of the two figures and add them together.

Area triangle = $\frac{1}{2}b \times h = \frac{1}{2}(32 \times 32) = 512$ square units

Area rectangle = $b \times h = 20 \times 32\sqrt{2} = 640\sqrt{2}$ square units

Total area = $512 + 640\sqrt{2}$ square units

29. In the figure, $\triangle RST$ has been dilated by a factor of 2. If the coordinates of R are $(-1,-4)$, what are the coordinates of R'?

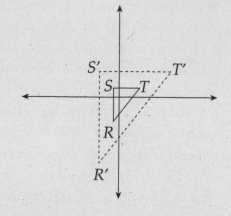

A. $(-3,-12)$

B. $(-12,-3)$

C. $(-1,-4)$

D. $(-2,-8)$

D. is the correct answer. To perform a dilation, simply multiply the original coordinates by the dilation factor to compute the coordinates of the dilated image.

30. The figure shows three regular pentagons. What is the sum of angles x, y, and z?

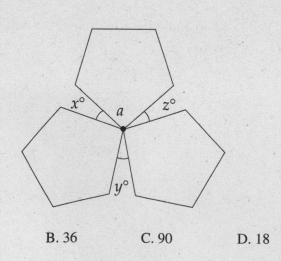

A. 120   B. 36   C. 90   D. 18

B. is the correct answer. Since the pentagons are regular, you know that each angle of the pentagon is $108°$ ($108 = 180(5 - 2)/5$). Since you know that the total degree measure around point A is $360°$, and there are three pentagons with each pentagon angle at $108°$.

$108° \times 3 = 324°$. Therefore, the sum of angles x, y, and z equals $360° - 324° = 36°$.

TEST THREE, DAY TWO

1. In the figure, $\overline{EB}$ is parallel to $\overline{DC}$. What is the value of $x + y$?

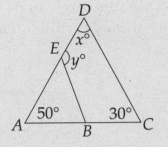

This is a surprisingly easy question. No calculation is involved. Since we know that $\overline{EB}$ is parallel to $\overline{DC}$, and $\overline{ED}$ cuts through them, $x + y = 180°$.

2. What is the value of $\angle x$ to the nearest tenth?

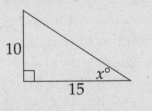

33.7 is the correct answer. $\tan x$ = opposite/adjacent, so:

$\tan x = 10/15$

$x = \tan^{-1}(10/15)$

$x \approx 33.7$

3. What is the area of the isosceles trapezoid in the figure (in square units)?

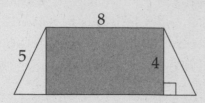

44 is the correct answer. Since you are not given the length of both bases, you have to be creative in solving this problem. Since the trapezoid is isosceles, the figure can be split into a rectangle and a isosceles triangle without changing the area:

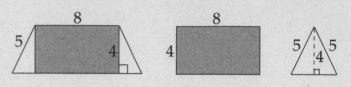

The area of the trapezoid equals the area of the rectangle plus the area of the triangle. The area of the rectangle is: 32 square units (8 × 4).

Next, in order to compute the area of the triangle, we need the length of the base. Notice that the triangle is split into two right triangles, each with a hypotenuse of 5, and one leg equals 4. Using the Pythagorean Theorem (or recognizing them as 3-4-5 right triangles), we know that the length of the other leg is 3. So, the length of the base of the triangle is 3, and the height is 4. So, the area of the triangle is 6 square units (1/2(3 × 4)).

Area of the trapezoid: 32 + 6 + 6 = 44 square units

4. What is the perimeter of a rectangle created by the *x*-axis, *y*-axis, and the point (–7,–4)?

(–7,4)

22 is the correct answer. You don't even need to use the distance formula to see that the length is 7 units, and the width is 4 units. Since the perimeter of a rectangle is $2 \times (l + w)$, the perimeter of this rectangle is $2 \times (7 + 4)$, or 22 units.

5. What is the volume (in square units) of a square building of side 12 with a pyramid roof with a slant height of 14 (to the nearest whole unit)?

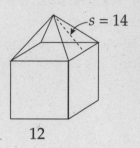

The correct answer is 1,879.

The building has two shapes to it: a cube and a pyramid. We need to find the volume of each and then add them together.

The cube is easy. Volume = s^3 = 12^3 = 1,728

The pyramid is a little trickier. The volume of a pyramid = 1/3(area of base) × height.

However, first you need to determine the height of the pyramid, because it is not given. To do that, analyze a cross-section of the pyramid:

14 — slant of pyramid

6   6
base of pyramid

The height of the pyramid bisects the base, which is 12, creating a right triangle with a hypotenuse of 14, and one leg is 6. The height is the other leg, and thus equals:
Height^2 = $14^2 - 6^2$
Height^2 = 196 − 36 = 160
Height ≈ 12.65
So, the volume of the pyramid is:
1/3 (12 × 12) × 12.65 × 607.2
Area of house ≈ 1728 + 607.2
2,335.2 ≈ 2335

Written Response Question

1. You open the can of soda in the figure below. By what percent is the total surface area decreased by opening it? Specify each idea you use.

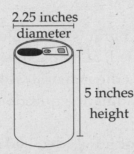

2.25 inches
diameter

5 inches
height

Note: Figure not drawn to scale.

height = 5 inches

diameter = 2.25 inches

diameter of circular opening = .75 inches

SAMPLE RESPONSE RECEIVING A SCORE OF 4

Surface area of cylinder = $2\pi r^2$ + (circumference × height)

SA of C = $2\pi(1.125)^2 + (\pi\partial \times 5)$

SA of C = $2(3.14)(1.27) + (3.14(2.25) \times 5)$

SA of C = $7.95 + 35.4$

SA of C = 43.29 square inches

Surface Area of opening = πr^2

SA of O = $\pi(\dfrac{.75}{2})^2 = .375$

SA of O = $3.14(.56)$

SA of O = $.442$ square inches

Total Surface area decreases by $.442/43.29 = .01 = 1\%$

This response is concise and complete. It accurately accomplishes the task and explains the steps taken and rules employed.

SAMPLE RESPONSE RECEIVING A SCORE OF 2

Can $= 2\pi(1.125)^2 + (\pi(2.25) \times 5)$

Can $= 43.31$

Opening $= \pi(.75)^2$

SA of $O = 1.76$

Can decreases by 1.76

All information in this response is correct, but it is incomplete, and does not accomplish the task at hand. The rules used are not specified, and no explanation is given. This is a good example of how someone who understands the material will not get full credit because of a lack of explanation, and carelessness in reading the question.

(Note: This is another classic example of how a detailed explanation will earn additional points. The student was one step from the final answer, but lost two valuable points because of the absence of explanation.)

PRACTICE TEST FOUR

SAMPLE MULTIPLE-CHOICE QUESTIONS FOR GEOMETRY

Make sure you have two or three No. 2 pencils with erasers and a ruler or straightedge available to you during the exam. You also may have a calculator; it may be either a scientific or graphing calculator. You may not use minicomputers, pocket organizers, or calculators with QWERTY (typewriter) keyboards. You may not share your calculator with other students.

Do not spend too much time on a question that seems too difficult. Answer the easier questions first and then return to the harder ones if you have the time. Try to answer every question, even if you have to guess.

Notes: (1) Figures that accompany problems are drawn as accurately as possible EXCEPT when it is stated that a figure is not drawn to scale. All figures lie in a plane unless otherwise indicated.

(2) All numbers used are real numbers. All algebraic expressions represent real numbers unless otherwise indicated.

TEST FOUR, DAY ONE

1. If the sum of all of the interior angles of a regular polygon equals 900°, how many sides does the regular polygon have?

A. 5   B. 6   C. 7   D. 8

2. What is the perimeter of this isosceles triangle to the nearest whole number?

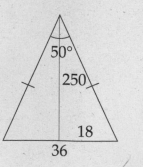

Note: Figure not drawn to scale.

A. 85   B. 121   C. 43   D. 156

3. What is $x + y$?

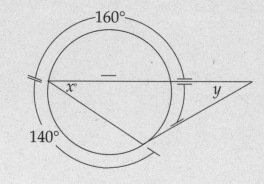

Note: Figure not drawn to scale.

A. 60°   B. 45°   C. 105°   D. 90°

4. What is the perimeter of the rectangle in the figure if ∠BAD = 40° and AD = 20 to the nearest tenth?

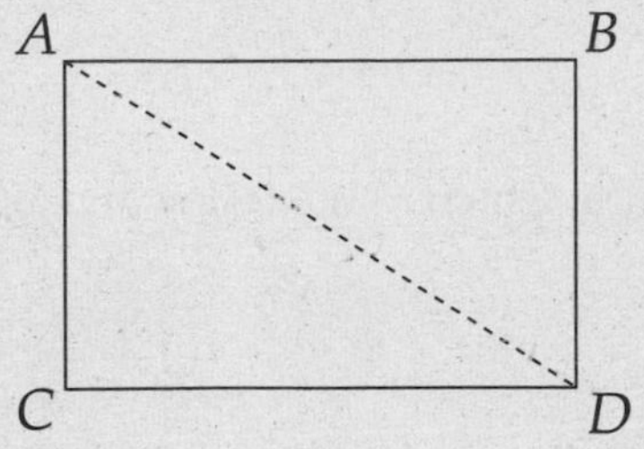

Note: Figure not drawn to scale.

A. 56.4   B. 197.0   C. 15.30   D. 28.2

5. What is the surface area of the following figure?

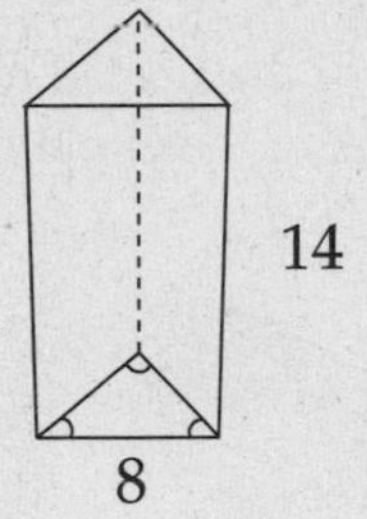

14

8

Note: Figure not drawn to scale.

A. 446   B. 391   C. 1240   D. 136

6. In the figure, which angle is congruent to 32°?

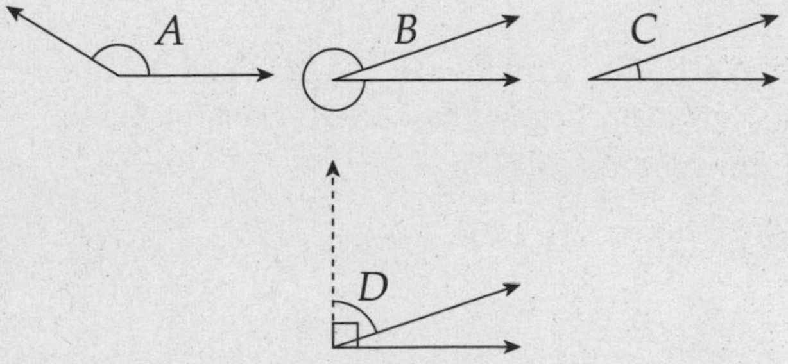

Note: Figure not drawn to scale.

A. A   B. B   C. C   D. D

7. Which shape best describes the figure made by these four points: (1,4) (3,2) (5,4) (3,6)

A. parallelogram

B. trapezoid

C. square

D. rectangle

8. If triangle ABC has 2 sides that measure $5\sqrt{2}$ and one side that measures 10, which degree measurement is one of the angles of the triangle?

A. 60   B. 45   C. 30   D. 50

9. If the perimeter of a two-dimensional shape is 50, what is the largest possible area the shape could have in squared units?

A. 156.25   B. 156.25π   C. 625π   D. 36π

10. What is the slope of a line which is perpendicular to the line defined by the points (−3,8) and (5,12)?

A. 2   B. −2   C. −.5   D. .5

11. What is the volume of the cylinder in the figure if the radius is 2.5 in cubed units?

13

A. 144π   B. 75π   C. 37.5π   D. 50π

12. In the figure, $\overline{AB}$ and $\overline{CD}$ are diameters of circle L. Measure of arc $DB = 55°$. What is the measure of $\angle ABC$?

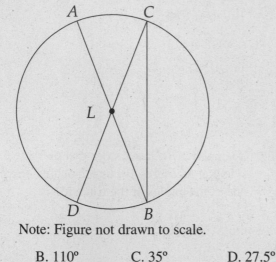

Note: Figure not drawn to scale.

A. 55°   B. 110°   C. 35°   D. 27.5°

13. If $\angle ABD$ and $\angle CBE$ are right angles, and m$\angle ABC = 20°$, what is the measure of $\angle DBE$?

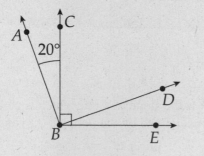

Note: Figure not drawn to scale.

A. 70°   B. 90°   C. 20°   D. 35°

14. In the figure, what is the length of b?

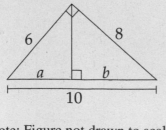

Note: Figure not drawn to scale.

A. 6.4   B. 4.6   C. 6   D. 4

15. What is the circumference of a circle whose center is located at (−6,9), and (4,4) is a point on the circle?

A. 71.47   B. 392.7   C. 70.24   D. 35.12

16. In the figure, which of the following could be AB?

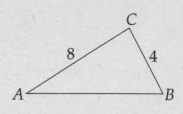

Note: Figure not drawn to scale.

A. 3   B. 6   C. 13   D. 32

17. What is the area of the shaded regions to the nearest tenth, if the radius of the circle is 10 in squared units?

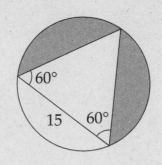

Note: Figure not drawn to scale.

A. 216.8   B. 97.4   C. 144.5   D. 289.0

18. $\triangle A'B'C'$ is a rotation of $\triangle ABC$ about the origin. How many degrees has $\triangle ABC$ been rotated to produce $\triangle A'B'C'$?

A. 90°   B. 180°   C. 270°   D. 360°

19. If the volume of a pyramid with a square base is 64 and its height is 12, what is the length of one side of the base?

A. 24   B. 2.4   C. 4   D. 3.2

20. What is the height of the triangle in the figure?

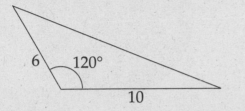
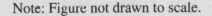

Note: Figure not drawn to scale.

A. $6\sqrt{3}$

B. $3\sqrt{3}$

C. $10\sqrt{3}$

D. $2\sqrt{15}$

21. The figure shows an isosceles triangle inside a regular pentagon. What is the degree measure of x?

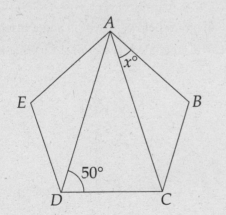

Note: Figure not drawn to scale.

A. 14   B. 22   C. 36   D. 50

22. Lines a and b are parallel. Which of the Congruence Theorems prove that triangle ABC and triangle DEC are congruent?

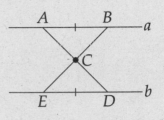

Note: Figure not drawn to scale.

A. SSS   B. ASA   C. SSA   D. AAS

23. What polygon is created by the lines $3x + y + 3 = 3(x + 1)$, $x + y = 4$, the x-axis, and the y-axis?

A. triangle

B. square

C. trapezoid

D. parallelogram

24. What is the area of the polygon in the figure in squared units?

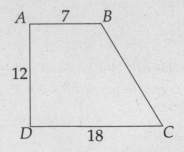

Note: Figure not drawn to scale.

A. 84   B. 66   C. 5,544   D. 150

25. In the figure, $\overline{AD}$ and $\overline{EC}$ are diameters of the circle O, and $\overline{OB}$ bisects $\angle AOC$. What is the degree measure of arc AC?

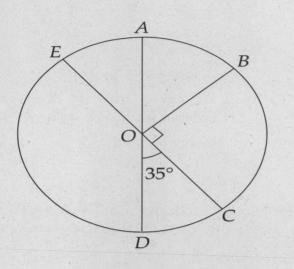

Note: Figure not drawn to scale.

A. 40   B. 70   C. 140   D. 110

26. What is the surface area of a regular triangle pyramid with a base side length of 12?

A. $72\sqrt{3}$ B. $72\sqrt{2}$ C. $169\sqrt{3}$ D. $144\sqrt{2}$

27. In the triangle ABC, the length of $\overline{AB}$ = 12, the length of $\overline{BC}$ = 8, and the length of $\overline{AC}$ = 15. Which angle is the largest?

 A. $\angle A$

 B. $\angle B$

 C. $\angle C$

 D. They are all the same

28. In the figure, what is the area of the shaded region (in square units) to the nearest tenth, if the radius of the inner circle is 10, the radius of the outer circle is 12, and the apothem of the octagon is 4.62?

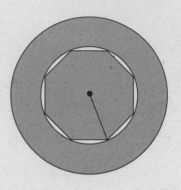

Note: Figure not drawn to scale.

A. 452.4   B. 314.2   C. 70.6   D. 208.8

29. What is the value of x?

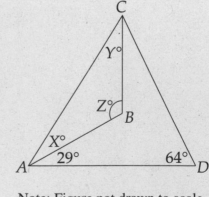

Note: Figure not drawn to scale.

A. 26°   B. 98°   C. 154°   D. 64°

30. In the diagram below, $\overline{AB}$ is an angle bisector of $\angle A$ and $\overline{CB}$ is an angle bisector of $\angle C$. What is the value of Z?

Note: Figure not drawn to scale.

A. 93   B. 128   C. 122   D. 87

SAMPLE GRIDDED-RESPONSE QUESTIONS FOR GEOMETRY

The following questions are similar to the multiple-choice questions, but answer choices are not provided. You must determine the answers yourself using separate scratch paper, and then use a special area on the answer sheet like the one shown here to bubble in your answers. If the answer is a mixed numeral, it is to be gridded as a decimal or improper fraction (e.g., 3 1/2 should be gridded as 7/2 or 3.5).

Grid your response to items #1 through #5 below. Use the decimal (.) or the fraction sign (/) if your answers require it.

Examples of how to grid your answers

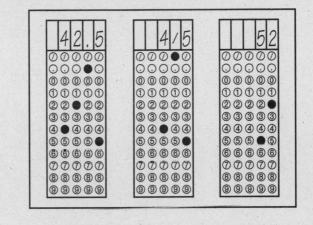

TEST FOUR, DAY TWO

1. If every angle in this diagram is at least 30°, what is the greatest possible value of x?

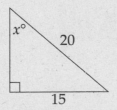

Note: Figure not drawn to scale.

2. What is the value of x to the nearest tenth?

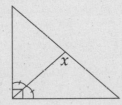

Note: Figure not drawn to scale.

3. In the figure, $\overline{AC}$ is a secant to circle O. What is the length of tangent $\overline{CD}$ to the nearest hundredth?

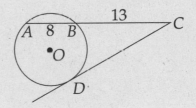

Note: Figure not drawn to scale.

4. What is the area of a circle whose center is located at $(-2,2)$, and $(-5,4)$ is a point on the circle (to the nearest tenth and in square units)?

5. What is the surface area of this regular hexagon prism to the nearest tenth (in square units)?

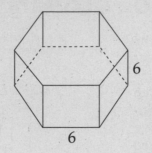

Note: Figure not drawn to scale.

Written Response Question

1. In the figure below, line *u* is parallel to line *v*. Explain how to find the measure of –x and the measure of –y. Specify each idea you use.

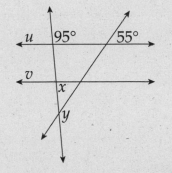

Note: Figure not drawn to scale.

Remember to show all parts of your solution, and explain how you arrived at your answer.

ANSWER KEY TO GEOMETRY PRACTICE TEST FOUR

Day One Questions: **Day Two Questions:**

Day One		Day Two

1 C

2 B   Grid-Ins:

3 C   1 105

4 A   2 48.6

5 B   3 16.52

6 C   4 40.8

7 C   5 403.1

8 B

9 C   Written Response:

10 B   1. See explanations for a properly credited response.

11 B

12 D

13 C

14 A

15 C

16 B

17 C

18 C

19 C

20 B

21 A

22 D

23 A

24 D

25 B

26 D

27 B

28 D

29 C

30 C

GRID-IN ANSWER SHEET

1 2 3 4 5

6 7 8 9 10

1

YOUR NAME: _____
(Print)
Last   First   M.I.

SIGNATURE: _____ **DATE:** ___ / ___ / ___

HOME ADDRESS: _____
(Print)
Number and Street

_____
City   State   Zip Code

PHONE NO.: _____
(Print)

Completely darken bubbles with a No. 2 pencil. If you make a mistake, be sure to erase mark completely. Erase all stray marks.

Practice Test Four

1. Ⓐ Ⓑ Ⓒ Ⓓ   16. Ⓕ Ⓖ Ⓗ Ⓙ
2. Ⓕ Ⓖ Ⓗ Ⓙ   17. Ⓐ Ⓑ Ⓒ Ⓓ
3. Ⓐ Ⓑ Ⓒ Ⓓ   18. Ⓕ Ⓖ Ⓗ Ⓙ
4. Ⓕ Ⓖ Ⓗ Ⓙ   19. Ⓐ Ⓑ Ⓒ Ⓓ
5. Ⓐ Ⓑ Ⓒ Ⓓ   20. Ⓕ Ⓖ Ⓗ Ⓙ
6. Ⓕ Ⓖ Ⓗ Ⓙ   21. Ⓐ Ⓑ Ⓒ Ⓓ
7. Ⓐ Ⓑ Ⓒ Ⓓ   22. Ⓕ Ⓖ Ⓗ Ⓙ
8. Ⓕ Ⓖ Ⓗ Ⓙ   23. Ⓐ Ⓑ Ⓒ Ⓓ
9. Ⓐ Ⓑ Ⓒ Ⓓ   24. Ⓕ Ⓖ Ⓗ Ⓙ
10. Ⓕ Ⓖ Ⓗ Ⓙ   25. Ⓐ Ⓑ Ⓒ Ⓓ
11. Ⓐ Ⓑ Ⓒ Ⓓ   26. Ⓕ Ⓖ Ⓗ Ⓙ
12. Ⓕ Ⓖ Ⓗ Ⓙ   27. Ⓐ Ⓑ Ⓒ Ⓓ
13. Ⓐ Ⓑ Ⓒ Ⓓ   28. Ⓐ Ⓑ Ⓒ Ⓓ
14. Ⓕ Ⓖ Ⓗ Ⓙ   29. Ⓐ Ⓑ Ⓒ Ⓓ
15. Ⓐ Ⓑ Ⓒ Ⓓ   30. Ⓐ Ⓑ Ⓒ Ⓓ

PRACTICE TEST FOUR
EXPLANATIONS

1. If the sum of all of the interior angles of a regular polygon equals 900°, how many sides does the regular polygon have?

A. 5   B. 6   C. 7   D. 8

C. is the correct answer. Remember that the equation for the sum of the interior angles of a regular polygon is sum = 180°($n - 2$), where n = number of sides.

$$900° = 180°(n - 2) \quad \text{Solve for } n$$

$$900 = 180n - 360$$

$$1,260 = 180n$$

$$n = 7$$

2. What is the perimeter of this isosceles triangle to the nearest unit?

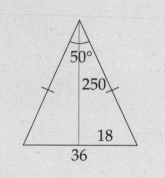

A.   85   B. 121   C. 43   D. 156

B. is the correct answer. First, draw a height for the triangle. Because this is an isosceles triangle, this line bisects the 50° angle, and it bisects the opposite side into two equal segments. Now, use trigonometry to solve for the length of the unknown sides (which are congruent):

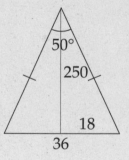

sin 25 = 18/hypotenuse
(hypotenuse)sin 25 = 18
hypotenuse = 18/(sin 25)
hypotenuse ≈ 42.6
perimeter ≈ 36 + 42.6 + 42.6
perimeter ≈ 121.2
Rounded to the nearest whole number, the perimeter is 121 units.

3. What is $x + y$?

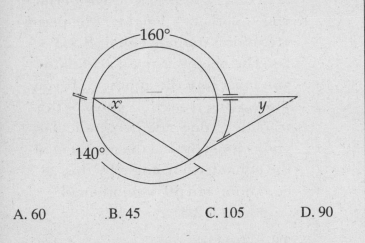

A. 60   .B. 45   C. 105   D. 90

C. is the correct answer. The arcs in a circle sum to 360°, so the arc subtended by $\angle x$ equals:

$$360° - 140° - 160° = 60°$$

Since $\angle x$ is an inscribed angle, it equals $\frac{1}{2}$ the measure of the arc it subtends: $\frac{1}{2}(60) = 30$.

$$x = 60°$$

The measure of an arc formed by a secant and a tangent equals $\frac{1}{2}$ the difference of the intercepted arcs.

So, $y = \frac{1}{2}(140 - 60) = 40$

$$y = 40°$$

$$x + y = 100°$$

4. What is the perimeter of the rectangle in the figure if $\angle BAD = 40°$ and $AD = 20$ to the nearest tenth?

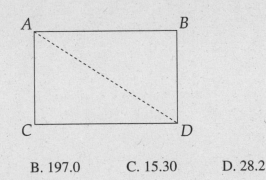

A. 56.4   B. 197.0   C. 15.30   D. 28.2

A. is the correct answer. This solution uses trigonometry.

$\sin 40° = BD/20$ $BD \approx 12.9$
$AC = BD \approx 12.9$

$\cos 40° = AB/20$ $AB = 15.3$
$CD = AB \approx 15.3$

The perimeter $\approx 2(12.9) + 2(15.3) \approx 56.4$

5. What is the surface area of the following figure?

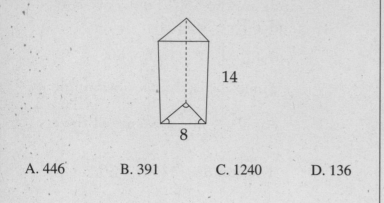

14

8

A. 446   B. 391   C. 1240   D. 136

B. is the correct answer. The surface area of a right prism equals perimeter (apothem + height). The perimeter of the triangle equals 8 × 3 = 24. The height is given = 14. Now you must find the apothem. If you draw a line from the center of the triangle to one side perpendicular, you can determine the apothem of the equilateral triangle by this equation: tan 30° = apothem/4. Apothem = 2.31

Therefore, the surface area of the right prism = 24 (2.31 + 14) = 391.

6. In the figure, which angle is congruent to 32°?

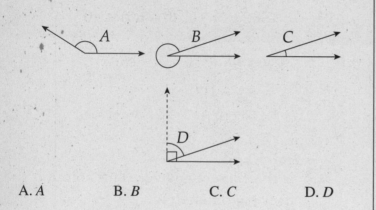

A. *A*   B. *B*   C. *C*   D. *D*

C. is the correct answer. *A* and *B* are obtuse angles, with an angle greater than 90°. *D* is greater than 45°, because it is larger than half of a right angle. *C* is the only possible answer.

7. Which shape best describes the figure made by these four points: (1,4) (3,2) (5,4) (3,6)

   A. parallelogram

   B. trapezoid

   C. square

   D. rectangle

C. is the correct answer. To verify that the figure is a square, use the distance formula to determine that the lengths of the sides are equal and use the slopes of the sides to determine that they intersect at right angles. (If a line has a slope of n, any line perpendicular to it will have a slope of $-1/n$.)

Distance formula:

$$\sqrt{(1-3)^2 + (4-2)^2} = \sqrt{8}$$

$$\sqrt{(3-5)^2 + (2-4)^2} = \sqrt{8}$$

(Repeat for the remaining sides.)

Slope formula:

$$\frac{2-4}{3-2} = -1$$

$$\frac{4-2}{5-3} = 1$$

(Repeat for the remaining angles.)

8. If triangle *ABC* has 2 sides that measure $5\sqrt{2}$ and one side that measures 10, which degree measurement is one of the angles of the triangle?

A. 60   B. 45   C. 30   D. 50

B. is the correct answer. In case you don't recognize this as a 45° right triangle, you could discover this by drawing the following triangle from the information given:

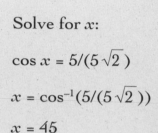

Solve for x:

$$\cos x = 5/(5\sqrt{2})$$

$$x = \cos^{-1}(5/(5\sqrt{2}))$$

$$x = 45$$

9. If the perimeter of a two dimensional shape is 50, what is the largest possible area the shape could have in squared units?

A. 156.25   B. 156.25π   C. 625π   D. 36π

C. is the correct answer. A figure with the largest area to the perimeter is a circle. The perimeter of a circle = $2\pi r = 50$; therefore, $r = 25/\pi$. You then plug that into the area equation. Area = $\pi r^2 = \pi(25/\pi)^2 = 625\pi$ square units.

10. What is the slope of a line which is perpendicular to the line defined by the points $(-3,8)$ and $(5,12)$?

A. 2   B. –2   C. –.5   D. .5

B. is the correct answer. Use the slope formula to determine the slope of the original line

$$\frac{y_2 - y_1}{x_2 - x_1} = \frac{12 - 8}{5 - (-3)} = \frac{4}{8} = \frac{1}{2}$$

The slope of a perpendicular is –1 divided by the slope of the line. Therefore, the slope of a perpendicular to this line is: –1/(1/2), or –2.

11. What is the volume of the cylinder in the figure if the radius is 2.5 in cubed units?

A. 144π   B. 75π   C. 37.5π   D. 50π

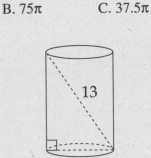

B. is the correct answer. The volume of a cylinder is $\pi r^2 h$. You are given the radius in the question. In addition, the figure shows a right triangle placed through the center of the cylinder. The side of the triangle which is located on the bottom of the cylinder is also the cylinder's diameter. So, you know that the length of that side is 5 (radius × 2). Since you are also given the hypotenuse of the triangle in the figure, you can figure out the height of the cylinder using the Pythagorean Theorem.

$$5^2 + h^2 = 13^2 \qquad h = 12$$

Now, you can simply plug in the numbers to find the volume.

Volume = $\pi r^2 h = \pi(2.5)^2(12) = 75\pi$ cubed units

12. In the figure, $\overline{AB}$ and $\overline{CD}$ are diameters of circle L. Measure of arc $DB = 55°$. What is the measure of $\angle ABC$?

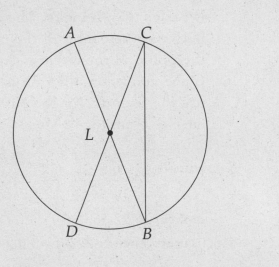

A. 55°   B. 110°   C. 35°   D. 27.5°

D. is the correct answer. $\angle DLB$ is a central angle, so it is the same as the arc it subtends, DB, and measures 55°. $\angle ALC$ is a vertical angle to $\angle DLB$, so it is also 55°. $\angle ALC$ is a central angle that subtends arc AC, so the measure of arc AC is also 55°. $\angle ABC$ is an inscribed angle that subtends arc AC, so it measures half the measure of arc AC:

$$\frac{1}{2}(55°) = 27.5°$$

13. If $\angle ABD$ and $\angle CBE$ are right angles, and m$\angle ABC$ = 20°, what is the measure of $\angle DBE$?

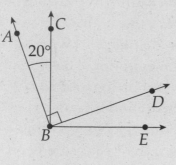

A. 70°   B. 90°   C. 20°   D. 35°

C. is the correct answer. m$\angle ABC$ + m$\angle CBD$ = 90°, so m$\angle CBD$ = 70°. m$\angle CBD$ + m$\angle DBE$ = 90°, so m$\angle DBE$ = 20°.

14. In the figure, what is the length of b?

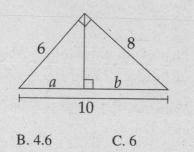

A. 6.4   B. 4.6   C. 6   D. 4

A. is the correct answer. Simply use trigonometry and algebra to solve for the length of b.

$$\cos x = 8/10$$

$$\cos x = b/8$$

$$b/8 = 8/10$$

$$10b = 64$$

$$b = 6.4$$

15. What is the circumference of a circle whose center is located at (–6,9), and (4,4) is a point on the circle?

A. 71.47   B. 392.7   C. 70.24   D. 35.12

C. is the correct answer. This problem is easier than it looks. The distance between the center of the circle and the point on the circle is the radius. Once you know the radius, simply use the formula for the circumference of a circle.

$$\text{radius} = \sqrt{(-6-4)^2 + (9-4)^2}$$
$$\sqrt{125} \approx 11.28$$
diameter $\approx$ 22.36
circumference $\approx$ 22.36 $\approx$ 70.24

16. In the figure, which of the following could be *AB*?

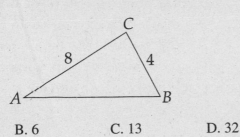

A. 3   B. 6   C. 13   D. 32

B. is the correct answer. Remember the rule regarding how long a side of a triangle can be: It can be no larger than the sum of the other two, and no smaller than the absolute value difference between them. For this triangle, the length is no more than 12 and no less than 4. 6 is the only number that fits.

17. What is the area of the shaded regions to the nearest tenth, if the radius of the circle is 10 in squared units?

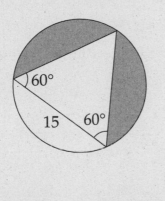

A. 216.8   B. 97.4   C. 144.5   D. 289.0

C. is the correct answer. To solve this problem, you will need the equation for area of a circle $(A = \pi r^2)$ and area of a triangle $(A = \frac{1}{2}bh)$. You will subtract the area of the triangle from the area of the circle, and then multiply that number by 2/3. The reason you multiply it by 2/3 is that the shading is only 2/3 of the total area calculated when you subtract the triangle from the circle. This is the case because the triangle is an equilateral triangle.   So let's do it:

Area of circle = $\pi r^2 = (10)^2 \pi = 100\pi \approx 314.2$ squared units

Area of triangle = $\frac{1}{2}(15)(7.5\sqrt{3}) \approx 97.4$ squared units

Area of shaded region $\approx (314.2 - 97.4)(2/3) \approx 144.5$ squared units

18. $\triangle A'B'C'$ is a rotation of $\triangle ABC$ about the origin. How many degrees has $\triangle ABC$ been rotated to produce $\triangle A'B'C'$?

A. 90°   B. 180°   C. 270°   D. 360°

C.   is the correct answer. Remember that positive rotations occur in a counter-clockwise fashion. (NOTE: −90° would also be a correct answer since negative rotations occur in a clockwise fashion.)

19. If the volume of a pyramid with a square base is 64 and its height is 12, what is the length of side of the base?

A. 24   B. 2.4   C. 4   D. 3.2

C.   is the correct answer. The equation for volume of a pyramid with a square base is volume = $1/3\ a^2h$,

so $64 = 1/3\ (a^2)(12)$

$a = 4$

20. What is the height of the triangle in the figure?

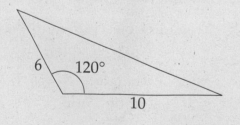

A. $6\sqrt{3}$

B. $3\sqrt{3}$

C. $10\sqrt{3}$

D. $2\sqrt{15}$

B.   is the correct answer. By drawing an external altitude, you create a 30-60-90 right triangle:

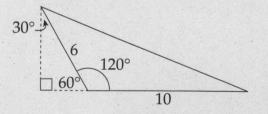

The side opposite the 60° angle is the hypotenuse × ($\sqrt{3}$)/2, so the altitude is $3\sqrt{3}$.

21. The figure shows an isosceles triangle inside a regular pentagon. What is the degree measure of x?

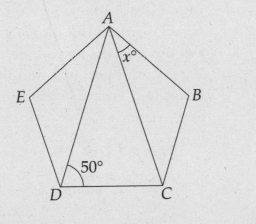

A. 14 B. 22 C. 36 D. 50

A. is the correct answer. In order to find the measure of angle x, first you need to find the measure of $\angle ABC$ and $\angle BCA$, and then m$\angle x$ + m$\angle ABC$ + m$\angle BCA$ = 180°.

You know m$\angle ABC$ = 108°, since the pentagon is regular, each angle of the pentagon is 180(5–2)/5 = 108°.

You are given $\angle ADC$, and since the triangle is isosceles, you know that m$\angle DCA$ also = 50°. Therefore, m$\angle BCA$ = m$\angle DCB$ (108°) – m$\angle DCA$ (50°) = 58°.

Now, you can calculate the degree measure of $\angle x$.

m$\angle x$ = 180° – (m$\angle ABC$ + m$\angle BCA$) = 180° – (108° + 58°) = 14°

22. Lines a and b are parallel. Which of the Congruence Theorems prove that triangle ABC and triangle DEC are congruent?

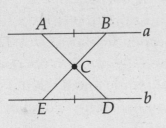

A. SSS B. ASA C. SSA D. AAS

D. is the correct answer. First, you know that $\angle BCA$ and $\angle DCE$ are congruent because vertical angles are congruent. Next, you know that $\angle CBA$ and $\angle CED$ are congruent because when a line (BE) passes through two parallel lines, alternate interior angles are congruent. Finally, you are given that $\overline{BA}$ and $\overline{DE}$ are congruent. Angle-angle-side is the theorem you want to use.

23. What polygon is created by the lines $3x + y + 3 = 3(x + 1)$, $x + y = 4$, the x-axis, and the y-axis?

A. triangle

B. square

C. trapezoid

D. parallelogram

A. is the correct answer. Don't let the four lines given to you fool you into believing that the figure will have four sides. In fact, $3x + y + 3 = 3(x + 1)$ is the same as $y = 0$, which is the same as the x-axis. So, graph $x + y = 4$, and you will find that a triangle is created with the x-axis and y-axis.

$$x + y = 4$$

$$y = -x + 4$$

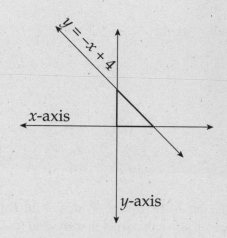

24. What is the area of the polygon in the figure in squared units?

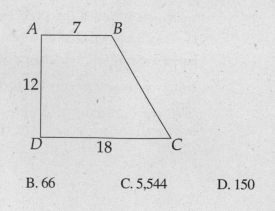

A. 84   B. 66   C. 5,544   D. 150

D. is the correct answer. To answer this question, first draw a line from B perpendicular to DC. That splits up the polygon into two easy figures: a rectangle and a triangle. From there, you can easily calculate the area.

Area rectangle = $l\,w = 12 \times 7 = 84$ squared units

Area triangle = $\frac{1}{2}\,bh = \frac{1}{2}(11)(12) = 66$ squared units

Total area = $84 + 66 = 150$ squared units

25. In the figure, $\overline{AD}$ and $\overline{EC}$ are diameters of the circle O, and $\overline{OB}$ bisects $\angle AOC$. What is the degree measure of arc BC?

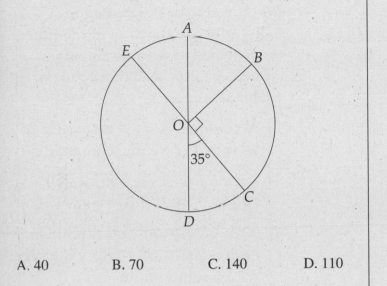

A. 40   B. 70   C. 140   D. 110

B. is the correct answer. $\angle DOA$ and $\angle AOC$ are supplementary, so $m\angle AOC = 180° - 40° = 140°$. Since OB is a bisector of $\angle AOC$, then $m\angle BOC$ is half of $m\angle AOC$, or $70°$. Since $\angle BOC$ is a central angle, the arc it subtends, the measure of BC, is also $70°$.

26. What is the surface area of a regular triangle pyramid with a base side length of 12?

A. $72\sqrt{3}$ B. $72\sqrt{2}$ C. $169\sqrt{3}$ D. $144\sqrt{2}$

D. is the correct answer. A regular triangle pyramid is one that has an equilateral triangle as a base, and three equilateral triangles for sides. The surface area of this figure is 4 times the area of the base. Since the altitude of an equilateral triangle is the length of the base times $\sqrt{3/2}$, the altitude of the basal triangle is $6\sqrt{3}$. The surface area of the pyramid is 4 × (1/2) (12) (6) = $144\sqrt{3}$.

27. In the triangle ABC, the length of $\overline{AB} = 12$, the length of $\overline{BC} = 8$, and the length of $\overline{AC} = 15$. Which angle is the largest?

    A. $\angle A$

    B. $\angle B$

    C. $\angle C$

    D. They are all the same

B. is the correct answer. The angle whose opposite side is the largest is also the largest angle. Think of it this way: If you are going to eat something, you need to put the food into your mouth. The wider you open your mouth, the larger the food can be that you put into it.

28. In the figure, what is the area of the shaded region to the nearest tenth, if the radius of the inner circle is 10, the radius of the outer circle is 12, and the apothem of the octagon is 4.62?

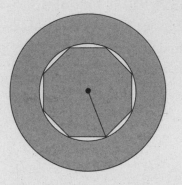

A. 452.4   B. 314.2   C. 70.6   D. 208.8

D. is the correct answer. Take this problem in steps. First, find the area of the outer circle. Then find the area of the inner circle. Next, find the area of the pentagon. Finally, subtract the area of the inner circle from the area of the outer circle, and then add that to the area of the pentagon.

1) Area outer circle = $\pi r^2 = \pi 12^2 = 144\pi \approx 452.4$ square units

2) Area inner circle = $\pi r^2 = \pi 10^2 = 100\pi \approx 314.2$ square units

3) Area pentagon = 1/2 (apothem × perimeter) = 1/2 (4.62 × 30.59) ≈ 70.6 square units

How did we get the perimeter? If you draw a line from the center to one corner (which also happens to be the radius of the circle = 5), and then draw the apothem, you can use the Pythagorean Theorem to find the length of half a side, and then you just multiply that by 16 to find the perimeter.

4) Area outer circle – area inner circle + area pentagon = 452.4 – 314.2 + 70.6 ≈ 208.8 square units

29. What is the value of x?

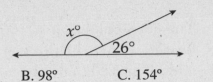

A. 26°   B. 98°   C. 154°   D. 64°

30. In the diagram below $\overline{AB}$ is the angle bisector of $\angle A$ and $\overline{CB}$ is an angle bisector of $\angle C$. What is the value of Z?

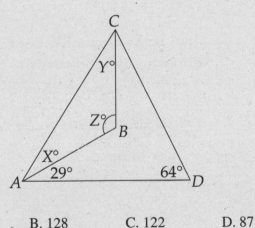

A. 93   B. 128   C. 122   D. 87

C. is the correct answer. The sum of supplementary angles equals 180°.
$180 - 26 = 154.\overline{CB}$

C. is the correct answer. The angles created by an angle bisector are equal, so m$\angle x$ = 29°. Also, m$\angle A$ = 58°. The angles in a triangle sum to 180°, so m$\angle C$ = 180 − 64 − 58, or 58. m$\angle Y$ equals half of m$\angle C$, so it is 29°. Z = 180 − 29 − 29, or 122.

TEST FOUR, DAY TWO

1. If every angle in this triangle is at least 30°, what is the greatest possible value of *x*?

    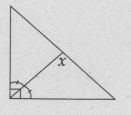

    The correct answer is 105°. Since we know that the three angles must add up to 180°, and the smallest value of *y* is 30°, $x = 180° - 45° - 30° = 105°$.

2. What is the value of *x* to the nearest tenth?

    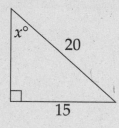

    48.6 is the correct answer. $\sin x = $ opposite/hypotenuse, so:

    $$\sin x = 15/20$$
    $$x = \sin^{-1}(15/20)$$
    $$x \approx 48.6$$

3. In the figure, $\overline{AC}$ is a secant to circle O. What is the length of tangent $\overline{CD}$ to the nearest hundredth?

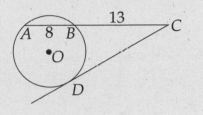

16.52 is the correct answer. Given a point exterior to a circle, the square of the tangent is equal to the product of the secant and the external segment. For this circle, it would be:

$$CD^2 = 13 \times (13 + 8)$$
$$CD^2 = 13 \times 21$$
$$CD^2 = 273$$
$$CD = \sqrt{273} \approx 16.52$$

4. What is the area of a circle whose center is located at $(-2,2)$, and $(-5,4)$ is a point on the circle (to the nearest tenth) in square units?

40.8 is the correct answer. This problem is easier than it looks. The distance between the center of the circle and the point on the circle is the radius. Once you know the radius, simply use the formula for the area of a circle.

$$\text{radius} = \sqrt{(-2-(-5))^2 + (2-4)^2}$$
$$= \sqrt{9+4} = \sqrt{13}$$
$$\text{area} = \pi r^2 = 13\pi \approx 40.8 \text{ square units}$$

5. What is the surface area of this regular hexagon prism to the nearest tenth (in square units)?

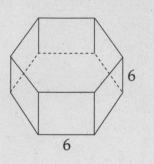

The correct answer is 403.1.
The surface of the hexagon consists of two regular hexagons (the top and the bottom of the prism), with sides that measure 6 units, and 6 squares (the sides of the prism), with sides that measure 6 units. You need to use right triangles to solve for the length of the apothem of the hexagon, which you will need to determine the area of the hexagon.

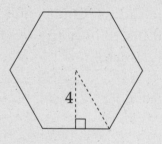

In this illustration, the apothem bisects one of the sides of the hexagon, and the line drawn to the angle from the center bisects that angle. The angle of a regular hexagon equals 120° (1/6 × 4 × 180).

So, the new angle is 60°, and this knowledge can be used to discover the length of the apothem:

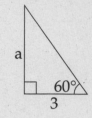

Because it is a 30-60-90 right triangle, you know that the length of the apothem is $3\sqrt{3}$. So, the area of the hexagon is

$\frac{1}{2}$(apothem)(Perimeter):

$\frac{1}{2}(3\sqrt{3})(6 \times 6) = 54\sqrt{3}$

Two hexagons = $108\sqrt{3}$ square units

The area of one square = 6 × 6 = 36

Area of all 6 squares = 36 × 6 = 216

Total surface area of the prism = $108\sqrt{3}$ + 216 ≈ 403.1 square units

Written Response Question

1. In the figure below, line u is parallel to line *v*. Explain how to find the measure of ∠*x* and the measure of ∠*y*. Specify each idea you use.

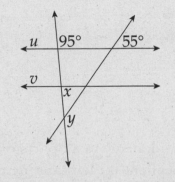

Remember to show all parts of your solution, and explain how you arrived at your answer.

SAMPLE RESPONSE RECEIVING A SCORE OF 4

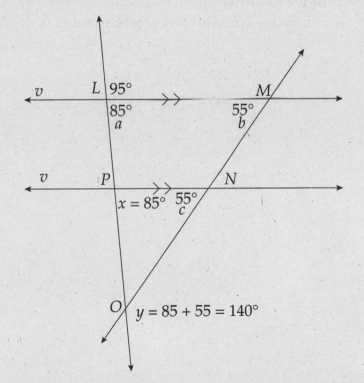

The 95° angle and $\angle a$ are supplementary angles;

$\therefore\ 95° + \angle a = 180°$

$\therefore\ \angle a = 85°$

$\angle a$ and $\angle x$ are corresponding angles of similar triangles ($\triangle LMO$ is similar to $\triangle PNO$)

$\therefore\ \angle a = \angle x$

$\therefore\ \angle x = 85°$

$\angle b$ and the 55° angle are vertical angles.

$\therefore\ \angle b = 55°$

$\angle y$ is an external angle to $\triangle LMO$

$\therefore\ \angle y = 180° - 85° - 55°$

$\angle y = 40°$

This response is clear and concise and answers all parts of the question. All rules are indicated, and the student displayed excellent understanding of the material by completing the task in the fewest steps possible, while fully explaining all manipulations.

SAMPLE RESPONSE RECEIVING A SCORE OF 2

x and the 95° angle are supplementary, so $x = 85°$

$y = 180 - 85 - 55 = 40°$

This brief response does not merit more than 2 points. Inaccurate use of the term "supplementary"(the two angles mentioned are not adjacent angles), and the complete absence of explanation for the determination of angle y illustrates how over-explaining is better than under-explaining.

ABOUT THE AUTHORS

Oliver Butterick recently received his BA in Philosophy at the University of California, San Diego. Oliver has professionally tutored math students between the fourth and ninth grades, and his passion for education is leading him to pursue his California teaching credential and an advanced degree in Education. When not advancing his own education or the education of others, Oliver plays roller hockey and ponders the role of government in our society (though not usually at the same time).

Rick Sliter joined The Princeton Review in 1994 after graduating with a degree in Quantitative Economics and Decision Sciences at the University of California, San Diego. Rick worked in two California offices, recently serving as Executive Director of The Princeton Review in Palo Alto.

Nationally, Rick has served on research and development teams to produce course materials for the SAT-I, SAT-II, and GMAT. This is his second series of books published by The Princeton Review. In 1998, he wrote *Cracking the CBEST*, a guide to help aspiring teachers in California pass the CBEST exam.

Rick currently lives in Los Angeles, pursuing a MBA at the Anderson School at UCLA.

FIND US...

International

Hong Kong
4/F Sun Hung Kai Centre
30 Harbour Road, Wan Chai,
Hong Kong
Tel: (011)85-2-517-3016

Japan
Fuji Building 40, 15-14
Sakuragaokacho, Shibuya Ku,
Tokyo 150, Japan
Tel: (011)81-3-3463-1343

Korea
Tae Young Bldg, 944-24,
Daechi- Dong, Kangnam-Ku
The Princeton Review- ANC
Seoul, Korea 135-280,
South Korea
Tel: (011)82-2-554-7763

Mexico City
PR Mex S De RL De Cv
Guanajuato 228 Col. Roma
06700 Mexico D.F., Mexico
Tel: 525-564-9468

Montreal
666 Sherbrooke St.
West, Suite 202
Montreal, QC H3A 1E7 Canada
Tel: (514) 499-0870

Pakistan
1 Bawa Park - 90 Upper Mall
Lahore, Pakistan
Tel: (011)92-42-571-2315

Spain
Pza. Castilla, 3 - 5° A, 28046
Madrid, Spain
Tel: (011)341-323-4212

Taiwan
155 Chung Hsiao East Road
Section 4 - 4th Floor,
Taipei R.O.C., Taiwan
Tel: (011)886-2-751-1243

Thailand
Building One, 99 Wireless Road
Bangkok, Thailand 10330
Tel: (662) 256-7080

Toronto
1240 Bay Street, Suite 300
Toronto M5R 2A7 Canada
Tel: (800) 495-7737
Tel: (716) 839-4391

Vancouver
4212 University Way NE,
Suite 204
Seattle, WA 98105
Tel: (206) 548-1100

National (U.S.)
We have over 60 offices around the U.S. and
run courses in over 400 sites. For courses and locations
within the U.S. call 1 (800) 2/Review and you will be
routed to the nearest office.